EXPECTATIONS
AND POSSIBILITIES

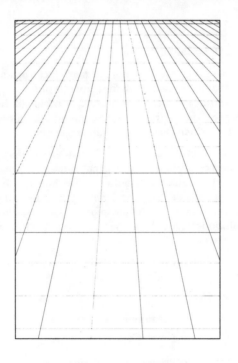

JOE D. BATTEN

 HAY HOUSE, INC.
Santa Monica, CA

EXPECTATIONS AND POSSIBILITIES

by Joe D. Batten

Library of Congress Catalog Number: 90-80053
ISBN: 0-937611-89-1

90 91 92 93 94 95   7 6 5 4 3 2 1

Original Hardcover Edition, First Printing, 1981
by Addison-Wesley Publishing Company

Trade Paperback Reprint, First Printing, June 1990
by Hay House, Inc.

Published and distributed in the United States by:

Hay House, Inc.
501 Santa Monica Blvd.
Post Office Box 2212
Santa Monica, California 90406 USA

Printed in the United States of America

FOREWORD

A book by Joe Batten is always an exciting event, and I think the title of his new book is even doubly exciting—*Expectations and Possibilities*. The very title suggests a positive attitude. One expects, anticipates, and believes that great things can take place, and he lives accordingly in the climate of possibilities. This creates an attitude in which results accrue that ordinarily might not come to pass.

Mr. Batten points out that all too often we allow other people to exercise direction for us and thereby actually define what we are or may become. The author feels that, as individuals, we need to be definitive about ourselves by the expectations we hold as to our own future—what we may become and do. Moreover, he points out that one of the best ways to express the love which we are supposed to have for our neighbors is to help other people to discover, form, and realize their own expectations. The author feels that none of us should ever allow ourselves to be shackled or compressed by what other people direct us to do.

Mr. Batten believes that the most important resource in life is people and that everyone needs to develop a clear and complete and rational system of expectations to set free the strength and power of the built-in resources which God has put into human life. Though Mr. Batten is not a preacher, as is this writer, he seems to have a spiritual text undergirding his material and it is a truly great spiritual word:

Ask, and it shall be given you;
Seek, and ye shall find;
Knock, and it shall be opened unto you.   (*Matthew 7:7*)

He believes that what he calls the expective pattern of living is God-given and is clearly outlined for us through the message and teachings of Jesus Christ.

Mr. Batten enunciates a very profound psychological truth—that we tend to become, at least, precisely what we expect. This, of course, is another way of stating the power of the creative image. What we picture in the mind, if it is long held, strongly tends to be reproduced in fact. If the expectation is good, it will produce good results.

To my knowledge, no one has handled the matter of expectation and possibility quite so comprehensively, explicitly, and directly as Joe Batten has done in this fascinating book. There is a strong motivational emphasis wedded to practicality that should make this book a valuable thinking and working companion for creative living.

Norman Vincent Peale

PREFACE

The courage to be. The courage to create. The courage to love, live, and grow toward the actualization of one's capabilities. These are the major components of the good life.

No one is perfect; indeed, all too few of us experience many moments of real excellence. Why the lives of quiet desperation we see around us? Why the pinched and pallid or bloated and florrid faces in the crowd—or in the mirror?

When we arrived on planet earth eons ago, it was a verdant place fraught with enormous possibilities. Much that is good, wonderful, and blessed has happened to the human condition. But we have fallen so pitifully short of our possibilities. We have become clothed, swathed, shackled, and stifled—all too often killed—by our attitudes.

Our attitudes are at the core of our being. They condition our biological anatomy, the activation of our brain cells, our choice of nutrition and exercise and, ergo, the condition of our bodies. They condition our relationships with others. They are truly the agents of change and arbiters of the quality of our lives.

Interestingly, our libraries and other repositories of learning contain ample information for the strengthening, toughening, and continued growth of attitudes that are good, right, powerful, and joyful. We all need a clearly charted *growth path* with clearly understood points on the growth continuum that enable success to be nourished by success.

A scale—a continuum—of *hope*, guided and stimulated by expectations. This is the intent of this book.

My wife, Jean, an extraordinary lady, who proofed the manuscript critically and caringly, and my daughters, Gail and Wendy, have made a far deeper impact on the great things that have happened in my life than I can possibly express.

Long-time colleagues like Hal Batten, Jim Swab, and Leonard Hudson have been valuable mainstays, friends, and sources of strength. A particular note of thanks goes to that consummate professional executive, John Wade, whose dedication, diligence, and loyalty is like a rock.

As we are increasingly blessed with a corporate reach that influences tens of thousands—perhaps millions—each year, the author must not only say, "My cup runneth over" but, "It splasheth."

Expect the best!

J.D.B.

Des Moines
December 1980

INTRODUCTION

KEEP REACHING—EXPECT THE BEST

In this book, it is my profound hope that each reader will discover new "possibility seeds," and that these seeds will sprout and flourish in the fertile soil of an expective lifestyle.

While leaders at all levels of organizational life may employ these principles in their jobs, this book is primarily about *how to live a life*—of growth, passion, empowerment, enrichment, purpose, and renewal . . . whoever you may be.

We have made incredible advances in high technology, but technology must always be secondary to human understanding and interpersonal relationships.

High-tech/high-touch must become high-touch/high-tech. The new frontier—the ultimate frontier—is and always will be the latent possibilities of *people*.

The broad sweep of this book is addressed to the betterment of society as a whole, not just the business community. Our focus here does not ignore the crucial role of the family. I believe that generation upon generation of dysfunctional families in all cultures of the earth are probably at the root of most of the manifestations of impaired relationships in all levels of our society . . even those between nations.

Throughout the world the sterility of communism is becoming obvious. Expectations and possibilities of 'the people' have already moved center stage. Military solutions pale in contrast with the ideas of positive, enlightened minds. Values . . . attitudes . . . positive actions . . . are the stuff of the future.

Thoughtful study and application of this book will enable the reader to make quantum leaps forward toward a stronger, more sensitive, creative, and thoroughly better self, and by extension, a better world.

If you, the reader, are somewhat fainthearted and "set in your ways"; if you want to settle for a safe, ordinary, and unnecessarily short life—beware . . . this book may stimulate a lot of changes . . . a lot of effort . . . a lot of growth.

If you're eager—or at least ready—for positive change, mental fitness, personal growth, and enrichment, read on. This may be the lifestyle for you.

In *Expectations and Possibilities* I've attempted to provide you with more than new insights and attitudes. There is a complete *system* of thought and action waiting for you to explore. Are you *tough-minded* enough to confront your possibilities? Do you dare to feel as good as you possibly can? If so, you may be on your way to becoming the *ultimate new you*!

Joe Batten
1990

CONTENTS

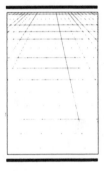

Part II
EXISTIVE MANAGEMENT ___ 71

Part I

EXPECTIVE LIVING

To provide excellence of expectations may be the finest
gift you can give another person.
Hope—the universal nourishment of the human being.
Expectations—steps on the path of hope.

All too often we let other people define us by their
directions or directiveness. Instead, we need to *define
ourselves* by our expectations of ourselves, our neighbors,
and our God.

One fine way of expressing love is to help others discover,
surface, and realize their expectations rather than to be

compressed and shackled by their internally or externally imposed directives.

Develop a clear and complete system of expectations in order to identify, evoke, and use the strengths of all resources in the organization—the most important of which is people.*

*Joe D. Batten, 1978, *Tough-minded management*, Amacom.

Chapter 1

ARE YOU DROWNING
IN FREEDOMS?

Are you really alive? Do you really know what you expect from yourself, from your friends and colleagues, from your loved ones, from events and circumstances? Where do you place your primary trust? Is it in others or in *you*?

What parts of you are simply *reacting* to what you think others want you to do and be?

Years ago I wrote a book called *Dare to Live Passionately* and in it I asked, "Can you dare to live with the flavor and thrill of total success as a total person?"

WHAT'S HOLDING YOU BACK?

From the time we are born, virtually all of us are informed in many ways what others want us to *not* do. We are informed in innumerable ways what others want us *to* be and do. Research tells us that by the age of twelve we have basically learned all the things we should *not* do—that from that time on, all the rest of the "shalt nots" in our lives are repetitive and redundant.

What we need so desperately is a greater knowledge of what *to* do. A sense and awareness of what to expect from ourselves and from every dimension of life itself.

During the last decade, we heard much of the "dropout," the persons who abandoned their families, their jobs, their education, essentially their *responsibilities*. This was done in countless ways encompassing excessive use of drugs, extreme asceticism, and other excesses of various kinds.

Fifteen years ago I devised and described a profile of a fictitious man I named Bert Farquhar. Here's the way he was described:

Let's take a look at Bert, how he lives, and a few things about him. Bert is forty-four and the head of a major unit in a medium-sized company. You can call it a bank, a store, or a manufacturing plant. He pulls into the driveway of a house that is better than the one in which he grew up. Sometimes he reaches—a little compulsively—for a drink as soon as he gets home; but at other times he doesn't need one at all. He usually is glad to get home, although he often paces restlessly about the living room, later in the evening. He doesn't know exactly why. He has some vague uneasiness and often becomes restless on Sunday because of a vague mixture of both dread and anticipation about going to work on Monday. He is getting a little thick around the waist. He finds he is increasingly wearing out the heels of his shoes rather than the front of them. He wonders from time to time whether his wife and family really love him or just the standard of living he provides. He is beginning to take note of every newspaper article about men who have heart attacks in their forties and fifties. He's a little puffy-eyed; he wonders whether the women still see him as a pretty virile and attractive guy. He vaguely yearns for a chance to prove it to a few of them. He has a good steak whenever he wants it. He buys good bourbon. He has two cars. His family does not lack any material necessity; indeed, they have a number of luxuries. He often has the feeling his subordinates are after his job and finds himself becoming defensive and/or sarcastic with them. Tensions develop—though never serious—between him and his boss. He can seldom put his finger on the reason for these tensions. He has vague fears and cannot identify them. He has become quite uncertain of what success really is! He is hungry for something, but he doesn't know what; he is tired. He may drop dead in a few years or in a few months. He has a better bank balance than he dreamed of when he was a boy. He has a better car, better home, and his children are going to better colleges.

What's missing? Real happiness, real success—that's what are missing!

Bert was—and is—a dropout. Strange term to describe a stereotyped image of modern respectability, job stability, community consciousness, and "successful" paragon of a "success-oriented" society? Not at all. The fact is that Bert is not really successful at all. He is drowning amidst abundant freedoms and because of a distorted notion of abundant freedoms. He is leading a life of what Thoreau called "quiet desperation." He is a victim of a *directive* society. He has experienced a plethora of "oughtness," of "shouldness." He has plenty to eat, plenty to drink, fine shelter, adequate financial security, and a respectable wife. He has two children who are properly clothed, fed, "educated," and who can look forward to a future of *more of the same.*

What does Bert need? Incidentally, "Bert" might mean *you* whether you are old, young, tall, short, male, female, black, red, yellow, white, Christian, Jew, Buddhist, or other.

First, let's list some things Bert *doesn't* need. These are *directive* actions, words, and concepts. Here they come—a myriad of them.

Push	Secondary purpose
Tell	Defensiveness and rote
Input	Caution
Compress	*Dissatisfaction*
Intended to guide	"*I want* you to. . . ."
Repress	Maintenance or erosion of motivation
Suppress	Accountability (when directed)
Depress	Invulnerable
Advise	Defensive
Impart	Discontinuity of achievement
Comply	Inconsistent motivation
Implode	Resistance
Contract	Expedience
Rigidity	"Do as I *say*. . . ."
Inward and down	Inflict motive on others
Static	Autocracy
Blunt	Cynicism
Convergence	Theory X
Take aim	Maintains
Replication of creativity	For getting
Anxieties	Compel
Repressed and glossed over conflict	Concern for active compliance

Manipulate	Resentful
Resignation	Retardation
Robot-like	Early obsolescence
Can't	Reduce
Don't	Couldn't
Won't	Wouldn't
Shouldn't	Didn't

Admittedly, some of these words may puzzle the reader. For instance, what might be wrong with the idea of "reduce"? I am listing it here in the context of directively imposed interpretations that equate reducing to narrowing or making smaller the dreams, hopes, experiences, goals, senses, and ergo *achievements* of our old friend, Bert Farquhar.

Note, please, that the *recipient* of these actions, words, and other kinds of communication feels directed and—all too often—emotionally drowned in the midst of the most free and opportunity-fraught nation in the world.

WHO'S STIFLING WHOM?

The recipient feels stifled in a host of subtle and not so subtle ways. All too often, unborn and stillborn expectations suffer an early demise in a sea of directives; well-meaning, loving directives, but nevertheless other-imposed wishes, desires, and requirements.

Early in my career, I remember coming out of graduate school with a newly awakened belief in myself. I visualized glittering opportunities ahead in contrast to earlier times spent in the Marines in World War II and several years of work as an hourly paid laborer. In these situations I usually was the recipient of many orders from highly directive supervisors.

My first job (with my freshly minted master's degree in my pocket) was as an executive trainee in a large retailing organization. The store manager was theory X, autocratic, a pusher and shover. In short, he was *directive*.

I was prepared to give this new employer my total commitment and effort. All that I had read and heard in advance had convinced me that here was a great organization and a fine future.

This commitment began to fade from day one (I didn't realize it then) when the store manager met with the eager, highly educated young trainee and began to use phrases like this:

"I want you to understand . . . ."
"I will personally direct your development."
"You shouldn't . . . ."
"You can't . . . ."
"You mustn't . . . ."
"Check with me—I won't let you foul up."
Ad infinitum, ad nauseam.

For six months I worked harder than I ever had in the Marines, on the farm, in the factory, the brickyard, and other "precollege" jobs. No matter how hard I worked and yearned for a compliment or an *expectation* of excellence, all I received was directives.

At the end of six months I resigned. What was happening, I now realize, was that my limitations were moving *in toward me*. What I subconsciously yearned for (as we all do) was to *expand toward my possibilities*.

THE RELATIVELY AFFLUENT DROPOUT

My colleagues and I work with a wide variety of people who "want" to succeed. One of our major concerns is to help them see the difference in simply *wanting* to succeed in a given endeavor and *deciding* to succeed. In order to *decide*, it is crucial that we carry out seven steps in the expective living process:

Get the facts.
Set specific goals.
Blend your skills, abilities, and talents.
Coordinate or mesh these elements.
Agree on what you will expect. Then decide.
Develop an action plan.
Control and monitor your progress.

Do Bert Farquhar and his innumerable male and female clones do this? They often believe they do. What really happens? Why do some researchers estimate that on the average we are using as little as 7 percent of our potential ability?

Our affluent society provides us with a vast assortment of opportunities, choices, and possibilities. Those crucial things that seem to be missing are simply missing in us. In the absence of sufficient self-esteem, self-confidence, feelings of significance, call it what you will, all too many of us flee from the sheer variety and abundance of secretly cherished options. Too many of us have been "pinched, pushed together, and shrunken" by overly generous doses of both "Thou shalt *not*" and "You ought to. . . ."

By the time Bert is in his late twenties or early thirties, he is thinking too much about his "niche," "slot," "role," or other euphemistic and pusillanimous synonyms for "casket." He, all too often, has begun to take quite literally the wry and wittily intentioned placebo known as the Peter Principle.

The president of a petroleum company came to see me several years ago. We had been drawn together by a mutual enjoyment of *The Lord of the Rings*, the great trilogy by J. R. R. Tolkien, and the great trilogy by C. S. Lewis about life in the corners of the universe called deep heaven, and *The Chronicles of Narnia*, also by Lewis. The president particularly enjoyed the classic *The Little Prince* by de St. Exupéry.

Privately, he wrote fiction, loved beautiful landscapes, words, and ideas and in myriad ways yearned to savor the flavor of each passing *now*.

But—and here is the strange, almost eerie thing he revealed—he said he had not dared to reveal these interests and talents to any of his colleagues or friends because they didn't "fit" the stereotyped role of a top executive. We discussed ways in which he could begin to clarify his expectations and translate them into action plans. He began to *be* rather than to feel constricted and limited to what he should *do*.

We hear much of the term "burnout" and it is often used in the context of "executive burnout," "worker burnout," and "parent burnout." Regrettably, this rather offensive term seems construed to be the result of too much work. I submit that this is seldom ever the case. The petroleum executive actually began to work harder than he had before. The "burnout" toward which he had seemed headed was primarily a cry from nature to become who he really was and could be—to reverse the insidious process of conforming to directives and begin moving toward expectives.

A basic point here is that he became significantly more *effective* as a manager, a parent, and a total person when he could reach beyond the cloying world of directives that had surrounded him like a sarcophagus and begin to realize his own unique expectations.

EXPECTATIONS AND HOPE

Hope is, indeed, the true nourishment of the person. Virtually *everything* that we do is fueled in some way by hope. Even bizarre, weird, and destructive actions are manifestations of warped notions that the result of those actions will fulfill the dream, goal, or wish *hoped* for.

All constructive and healthy plans, actions, and accomplishments are fueled by hope. It is the central elixir of life itself. Take away a person's hope and you have taken away the person's reason for living. You have taken away the person's basic motivation to play, work, love, care, share, and build.

Expectations are utterly and totally the stuff of hope. We can only express, target, and pursue hope through and by expectations. Earlier, I presented an assortment of directive words, actions, and concepts to illustrate environmental events that can shrink, constrict, erode and, in many cases, destroy hope.

Here's a list of expective words, actions, and concepts. Because we not only become what we think but also what we say, I hope you will think deeply about these expective elements.

Look forward	Count on
Hope	Prospective and perspective
Await	Future-oriented
Evoke	Predict
Unfold	Promise
Grow	Ask
Blossom	Create
Anticipate	Enthusiasm
Pull	Primary purpose
Lead	Vulnerability and openness
Output	Care
Lift	*Un*satisfied
Counsel	"Will you . . . ?"
Expand	Motive-ation
Explode	Accountability
Outward and up	Give
Dynamic	Share
Eager	Confront
Impatient and/or patient	"Follow me"
Foresee	The "we" feeling
Prepare for	Sense of wonder
Envision	Build
Apprehend	For giving

Catalytic action	Empathic
Candor	Concern for results
Surfaces conflict	Solves conflicts
Stimulate	Release
Respect	Renewal
Reciprocal response	Sensing
Reassurance of dignity	Exploration

For many years I've remembered and passed on to many people a tremendous quote from William H. Danforth's spendid little classic, *I Dare You!* Here it is.

I dare you, man of affairs, to have a "Magnificent Obsession."

Abraham Lincoln attended church one Sunday and heard a well-known minister who, many thought, was at the peak of his form because the President of the United States was in the audience. When asked what he thought of the sermon, President Lincoln said, "Since you've asked, I must confess I didn't think much of it." "Why?" he was asked. Lincoln replied, "Because he didn't ask us to do anything *great*."

SOME CHALLENGES

Do you care enough about you and your loved ones to put some *muscle* into your dreams?

Do you care enough to define *yourself*?

Do you care enough to *confront* your hopes?

Do you care enough to *ask* much from life?

Do you care enough to *build* "for giving" relationships?

Do you care enough to *seek* strengths in all things?

Do you care enough to replace cynicism with *wonder*?

Do you care enough to *eliminate* the apostrophe t's from your vocabulary?

Do you care enough to *share* the real you with others?

Do you care enough to distinguish between tranquility and *real* happiness?

Do you care enough to *lead*?

Expect the best!

Chapter 2

THE SPIRIT
OF ADVENTURE

*To exist is to snuggle
comfortably in the swaddling
clothes of the status quo.*

*To truly live is to confront
your possibilities.*

*Responsibility: The ability to fulfill one's expectations, and
to do so in a way that does not deprive others
of the ability to fulfill their expectations*

JOE D. BATTEN

The very anatomy of the word adventure fairly shouts *Expect!* Definitions include phrases like, "one who seeks . . .," "one that engages . . .," "an undertaking involving danger and unknown risk," "the encountering of risks," and "one who begins." And consider some definitions of spirit: "hope and apprehension of feasibleness," "an inclination, tendency, or impulse," "the activating or essential principle . . .," and "general intent or real meaning."

The very anatomy of the word spirit fairly shouts *Possibilities!* Let's begin to explore—to expect some insight—into the spirit of adventure.

QUESTING—STRETCHING

It was George Bernard Shaw, the salty, pungent individualist, who said:

You can see things that are, and you say, "Why?" but I see things that never were, and I say, "Why not?"

What other precedents exist for this massive, even awesome turn-about we are expecting? Did the great philosophers and leaders of history, the prophets of the great religions believe this? Let's examine a few and discuss their implications.

Aristotle said, "Lose yourself in productive work—in a way of excellence"; certainly a noble and lofty thought. Did he, however, understand practical matters, *action plans*? He also said, "Before we can do the noble, we must first do the useful."

Do you sense here any indication that he was urging us to wait for and respond only to the directives of others.

Plato addressed this question with such practical directness that it is truly exciting to think about. He gives us, in one sentence, the answer to many modern concerns such as how we can *influence* others; how we can *change* things; how we can leave the world better than we found it (a noble sentiment), and many more. Are you ready for all of this promised profundity? Here it is.

Before we can move the world, we must first move ourselves.

But, how do we *do* this? Where does the fuel come from? Can we, should we, wait for a directive? Another imposed direction? Who else really knows us? A homely, strong, and thoroughly American phrase we used to hear (and I yearn to hear it again) is "self-starter." Our next great philosopher is Socrates who spoke directly and practically to this need when he said:

Above all—know thyself.

OK, but how do we do *this*? Let's again move from the profound to the practical. First, we might say that "My self is the sum of you, me, and God." We might get a bit more specific and say, "You become what you think; you become what you say." Mahatma Gandhi, however, said it better than I have when he stated:

You will *find* yourself by *losing* yourself in service to your fellow man, your country, and your God.

Our individuality becomes etched out and confirmed as we *serve*.

SEEKING—SENSING

We're talking about the path of high adventure, about a spirit of daring, reaching, and above all *getting things done*—fulfilling expectations.

Interestingly enough, I propose to quote from a man, who is labeled a mystic by many, in order to illustrate the indivisibility of strong expective ideals and measurable, sense-able results. He is the prophet, poet, and philosopher Kahlil Gibran. I believe this to be one of the most sublimely meaningful statements of truth I have ever encountered. Gibran said:

> **Always you have been told that work is a curse and labor is a misfortune. But I say to you that when you work you fulfill a part of earth's furthest dream, assigned to you when that dream was born, and in keeping yourself in labor you are in truth loving life. And to love life through labor is to be intimate with life's inmost secret.**

Gibran may or may not have known that the word "work" appears in the Bible (I've been told) 564 times. It is in the daily arena of work, of daily interaction with the strengthening and testing realities of life that we truly find ourselves. In no sense, however, am I recommending a grubby, nitty-gritty preoccupation with work only for the sake of work. It is so crucial that these daily tasks be conditioned by purpose and direction— by the lifting, supportive pull of meaningful dreams.

One day in Boston I was presenting a seminar on "Tough-Minded Management," and at the coffee break a young manager said, "Joe, I had expected you to be an intensely practical guy, but I must say you sound to me more like an idealist." I said, "Thanks," and he quickly said, "I didn't mean that as a compliment. I paid to learn some *practical* management skills." With a smile, I said, "Would you mind picking up on this conversation with me when the day is over? I'd really like to know what you think then." He agreed and when the seminar was completed at about 4:30, we sat down together to talk some more. I will always remember the excellence and clarity with which he expressed his opinion. He said, with a happy look, "I think I've got it figured out. There's nothing more impractical than an idealist with *impractical ideals.* But, there's nothing more practical than an idealist with *practical ideals.*"

Perhaps Oliver Wendell Holmes meant something similar when he uttered this great expectation.

> **Will you look beyond the gold fields to the snowy heights of honor?**

He knew that a wise mix and blend of vision, dreams, action plans, and *work* was essential. B. C. Forbes, publisher of the eminently practical *Forbes Magazine* said it well.

> **Don't forget until too late that the business of life is not business, but living.**

TEACHING

Jaded, tired, dispirited teachers are all too commonplace. Most of them (us) mean so well and are the unwitting victims, to an extent that is at least amazing and at worst dreadful, of directive backgrounds, training, and other environmental factors.

As I seek to invite and challenge you to accompany me on the vicarious high road of expective reaching, we can, perhaps, again make effective use of some quotes from widely dissimilar sources.

First, the earthy, basic and very, very real poet Carl Sandburg.

Life is like an onion: You peel it off one layer at a time, and sometimes you weep.

How true! Notice carefully that he is not recommending that life should be lived in a fashion that would suggest that layer after layer of life be externally applied or plastered on in a safe and bland way. Yet, the common and prevalent approach to educating both young and old is to seek to *pour in knowledge*—to *directively influence* the learning process.

It is vital that we thoroughly retool our teaching techniques so that we evoke something *from* people rather than pouring something *into* them!

Our next quotable source is Jean Paul Sartre, a philosopher with whom I disagree on many points. Sartre does, however, make an excellent point with regard to expective teaching and education.

Each man must discover his own way.

It is important to stress that I am not recommending a purposeless, permissive, undisciplined approach. Rather, it requires *more* effort, *more* thought, *more* discipline, *more* trial and error, as well as obstacles and difficulties, to truly begin and follow through on an assessment of what you *can, should,* and *want* to expect from yourself in terms of learning, growth, and actualization.

ASKING

Alexis Carrel believed that nature should be asked all questions. He believed, and I believe, that one of our deadliest foes is the temptation to drown in directives and to lull ourselves with the self-proclaimed opiate that we have "arrived." We no longer are in a real state of flow. We have started to settle for answers in many phases of our life before we have truly begun to ask the real questions.

Frank Lloyd Wright, with tongue in cheek, said, "An expert is a man who has stopped thinking—he knows." I submit, in reality, that the art of asking questions adds spice, flavor, and zest to life. It will usually increase exponentially and synergistically—that is, the sheer momentum of insight stimulates an ever-increasing and healthy curiosity.

For example, a man I know, who is in many other respects a sage and wise person, has often assured me that he would not question the wisdom of his medical doctor—his M.D.—in any circumstances. My friend studiously ignores new literature on nutrition, fitness, stress management, etc. He has been directively influenced by over fifty years of being told (albeit subtly) of the infallibility of those who have taken the Hippocratic Oath.

Bertrand Russell speaks directly to this man's kind of mental myopia.

If fifty million people say a foolish thing, it is still a foolish thing.

Perhaps Thoreau said it even better.

Lo! Men have become the tools of their tools.

The Batten Prescription:

- If you don't know, ask!
- If you are unsatisfied, ask!
- If you want to lead rather than push or follow, ask!
- If you want to consummate a persuasive objective, ask!
- If you are tempted to respond to a situation with anger and a directive statement, ask!
- If you desire to communicate (shared meaning—shared understanding) rather than simply engage in dialogue, ask!
- When bored with directives and declarative statements, ask!
- When beset by confusion, ask!
- When you encounter hostility and passive resistance, ask!
- When you expect good things from life, ask!

Do you think it is a coincidence that three of the most powerful expectives in the history of humankind were worded in the following order?

Ask and it will be given you.
Seek and you will find.
Knock and it will open unto you.

The following poem by an unknown author speaks for itself.

I bargained with life for a penny,
And life would pay no more.
However I begged at evening,
When I counted my scanty store.

For life is a just employer.
It pays you what you ask,
But once you have set the wage,
Then *you* must bear the task.

I worked for a menial's hire,
Only to find, dismayed,
That anything I had asked of life,
Life would have willingly paid.

Chapter 3

WE BECOME WHAT WE EXPECT

*America is great because America has great
expectations. If America ceases to expect
greatness, America will cease to be great.*

JOE D. BATTEN

Let life *in* and let you *out*. We let life in by relating our expectations to
the world around us and the future as we anticipate it. We let ourselves
out—*TO BECOME*—as we focus on many other-directed things. Such
things include

Humor and laughter

Warm, reciprocal relationships

Good food and drink

Good books and conversation

Good ideas

Caring and sharing

Loving relationships

Hopeful relationships

Challenges and obstacles

Gratitude—felt and *expressed*

Compassion and empathy

Reinforcing strengths of self and
others

Eagerness for change

The joy of discovery

Perceived and zestful purpose

The joy of forgiving

The joy of building

A sense of wonder

The achievement of
goals—particularly when
self-generated

William Shakespeare appears to have thought and written more
about *becoming* and *being* than virtually anyone this side of the *Bible*.
For instance, when he wrote, "*To be* or not to *be*, that is the question,"
he was not simply perpetrating a homily for us to toss about vacuously
and in a humorously declamatory way. To *be is* the question! We are all
becoming . . . what? You alone can truly determine *that,* in relationship
to what you expect from God, your fellow person, and yourself.

Shakespeare had many other thoughts about being.

. . . sweet are the uses of adversity.

He knew that we can only discover, confirm, and etch out our selfhood—or being—when we reach *outward* to solve problems, to confront obstacles, and difficulties; to discover new strengths, skills, and possibilities. When we retreat into ourselves for *safety,* for low risk living, we begin to atrophy and die.

Shakespeare also wrote:

To thine own self be true. . . .

And here we confront the fact that we can build a life of reality only on a foundation of real or *truthful* relationships. We then perceive, further, that such interaction with the world around us is possible only if we are, first of all, in touch with and *true to ourselves.*

Here are some specific conversions—some specific ways—to move beyond mere existence toward really *becoming.*

From	*To*
Dissent	Protest
Greed	Gratitude
Getting	Giving
Hate	Love
Doubt	Faith or belief
Destroying	Building
Defensiveness	Openness and vulnerability
Aloofness and remoteness	Involvement
Hardness	Toughness
Violence and directiveness	Firmness and expectiveness
Self-diminution	Self-respect and dignity
Focusing on weaknesses	Building on strengths
Against	For
Negativism	Positiveness
Static	Dynamic
Pushing	Leading
Low expectations	High expectations
Rigidity	Flexibility
Grimness	Cheerfulness
Quantity	Quality

A stretching and transcendent goal etches out the reality and identity of the person.

To live with a sense of wonder may be the nearest thing to a full state of grace.

FULFILLING PROPHECIES

Why is this section not entitled, "*Self*-fulfilling Prophecies"? Simply because we live in a full and complete world of prophecies. There are many kinds other than self-fulfilling, although, of course, we condition these prophecies (or expectations) directly and indirectly by those we formulate for and about ourselves.

A dream is that most precious part of us that is personal, unique, and real. An objective is a dream with timetables and muscle.

The "ends" in our lives should condition the "means" or the methods.

Allow me to sketch out another profundity here, and then we'll discuss each of its four elements in terms of prophecies.

Faith, hope, and love are the real vitamins of the person.
Gratitude fuses these into a unified whole.

FAITH + HOPE + LOVE = GRATITUDE

Over the years I have counseled with many people who possessed financial affluence and emotional, mental, or spiritual poverty. In most instances, the principal things lacking were the four elements above. In a variety of ways, I have suggested the importance of feeling and expressing gratitude daily to others and to one's own conception of God. The atheist and agnostic pose special challenges here. But it is amazing how atheists and agnostics begin to formulate some notion of a meaningful Deity as they grow in their capacity to feel and express gratitude. It generates a *glow!*

The reader is invited to explore and challenge the following statement, which I freely admit sounds dogmatic and simplistic. But—please!—ponder it.

GRATITUDE AND DEPRESSION CANNOT COEXIST

Please also consider this next one, which may also seem rigid and/or oversimplified.

To allow yourself to exist in a poor state of physical fitness if there is no medical reason is to say to your creator: "I reject Your gifts. I do not appreciate them."

We set in motion a massive amount of prophecies that can and will feed back generous amounts of self-discovery, self-fulfillment, and self-actualization when we *invest* in generous portions of

Faith — To *believe* in people, events, relationships, in life itself, is to really live with every sinew, fiber, and erg of your being. A life of doubt and cynicism curdles, reduces, and sours.

Hope — Is the living twenty-four-hour-a-day evidence that we *count*, we are *real*, there is *good* in life. Expectations (prophecies) are usable instruments in each of our hope chests. Without hope we have no motivation to live, to work, to grow. There is, then, really *nothing*.

Love — Here is the healing, unifying, integrating, stimulating, renewing, reassuring, and constructive life force at the core of all good things. Without it, we have violence, destruction, confusion, and—you name it.

Gratitude — The great blender, it puts it all together. Gratitude provides us with specific ways of expressing faith, hope, and love and, perhaps more importantly, sets in motion a kind of reciprocity that further nourishes and increases the *amounts* of faith, hope, and love in one's life. Without it, our words, manner, and very appearance are a veritable "turnoff" to other people. The circle closes, becomes a vicious circle, and life loses all real zest, verve, and gusto.

How, specifically, do we go about launching the right prophecies for fulfillment? I'd like to introduce the following phrase as a way of describing a life-style:

SOWER OF EXPECTATIONS

This is obviously a variant of the great cybernetic statement, "As you sow, so shall you reap." We write our own destiny; we become what we expect, and then we become what we do. Every thought has a consequence; every cause has an effect. Always act as though you have already achieved what it is you want to achieve. (Think of this as you read the first of the two anecdotes at the end of this chapter.)

Let's examine some of these noble-sounding sentiments. How does it work?

First, recognize that two widely held notions of "goodness" and "propriety" often get in the way of real expective relationships. The first one is a perversion of the notion of "modesty." For instance, if you need an assignment or a request from me in order to carry out a necessary task, and I give you vague, tentative hints concerning what is desired because I don't want you to think that I think I'm "all that great," I am denying you not only clear shared meaning and understanding but I am also handicapping you in doing a good job. *I am letting you down.* My own lack of clarity, confidence, and purpose has been transmitted to you through a fuzzy filter of modesty and self-effacement.

Second, if I want everybody to always perceive me as "nice," I will usually express some indirect wishes to you rather than warm, clear, and—yes—often, *firm* expectations.

There are, of course, many other factors of mood, confidence, level of preparation, intent, etc. that serve to blur and obscure clear expectations.

To be sure that we "sow expectations" wisely, confidently, and clearly, it is crucial that we start with the person in the mirror.

Do *you*

	Yes	No
Know what you expect to become?	___	___
Know what reinforces and renews you?	___	___
Dare to feel as well as you possibly can?	___	___
Let yourself laugh with spontaneity?	___	___
Want lots of peace?	___	___
or		
Want lots of challenge?	___	___
Want a high measure of job success?	___	___
Want unity of mind, heart, and soul?	___	___
Want to discover new truth and beauty?	___	___
Want more self-confidence?	___	___
Want more self-understanding?	___	___
Want to live like a green, growing bud?	___	___
or		
Want to become a sapless autumn leaf?	___	___

Want to lead a quiet indwelling life?   ____ ____
Want to reach out into your entire environment?   ____ ____
Want to "look out for number one"?   ____ ____
Want to do a lot of caring and sharing?   ____ ____
Want to live behind a carefully controlled face?   ____ ____
Want to be vulnerable and open?   ____ ____

Develop some more questions unique to *you* and answer them?

	Yes	No
_____?	____	____
_____?	____	____
_____?	____	____
_____?	____	____
_____?	____	____

Once we begin to truly understand our self-expectations and discover that this is who and what and where we really are, it becomes *much* easier to begin to communicate expectively with others rather than directively or muzzily, fuzzily, abrasively, vaguely, shrilly, etc.

Here are some examples of ways to sow (and thus reap) expectations.

"Will you do it?"

"Please give me your opinion on this."

"OK, since we seem to be in full agreement on this, here is what I expect." (Quality, quantity, time, or target date)

"OK. I'll expect it by 9 A.M. tomorrow."

"OK. Let's do it!"

There is an infinite number of variations of the above. The central idea, however, is that when we request rather than command, we care enough to ask, get facts, listen, and above all, *hear*. We are speaking then to the dignity, worth, and individuality of the other person.

> **Note:**   I'll be repeating this in various ways in this book.

Expectations and firmness—caring enough to really mean it—are indivisible!

Expectives are *stronger* than directives! They get better results!

MUSCLE IN YOUR DREAMS

In the Education Division of our company, we present over 3,000 seminars a year in North America. Thus when we, the staff, sit down together to discuss some of the wants, needs, and problems of the thousands of men and women who attend, we are talking about a vast and highly diversified number of people.

Often in these seminars we find that the problem areas in the lives of these people defy precise definition. Here are a few.

"I can't motivate my people"

"My kids and I can't communicate"

"I've lost sight of the goals I had"

"I don't know what's happening to my time"

"I need more confidence"

"People don't listen to me"

"People don't understand me, and I don't understand myself"

"My husband (wife) and I can't communicate"

It can be readily perceived that the principal thing lacking in these lives—the vacuum at the center—is a dream. We must expect to lose ourselves in interests, causes, commitments, and ideas larger and more enduring than we are. We all need dreams, transcendent hopes, and expectations that subliminally flavor, season, and nourish all that we say and do. If that dream is made of happy expectations, it comes back to us like a boomerang, becomes a cybernetic circle.

Life is a mirror and gives back to each of us the reflection of our own self. Uncommon people—whether uncommon mechanics, admirals, doctors, machinists, executives, parents, or shepherds—can be products only of uncommon dreams.

We need tempo and pace in our lives. To be able to move from one point on life's continuum to the next in a fairly organized and purposeful way is important to vibrant, productive living. And all of this must be fed by a dream—a dream of what you want to do and be.

I have found in my own life that the moments of greatest productivity and accomplishment, although often hectic and frenetic, are those in which I have felt a rhythm and cadence. Rhythm and cadence can flow out of only a daily sense of purpose and direction.

Without purpose and direction you are like the guy who jumped on a horse and rode ten ways at once. Not only is it unproductive but it's *painful*!

What are *your* dreams? Shall we examine a few?

	For me	Not for me
To live with a sense of wonder		
To accumulate vast financial wealth		
To experience a high level of vitality—physical, mental, and spiritual		
To expect the best from every dimension of life		
To perceive the good—or the God—in everyone		
To *build*: with every thought, word, and action		
To live with vulnerability and grace		
To radiate enthusiasm		
To always live *now*		
To become what I *think* and *say*		
To live without stridency, shrillness, and defensiveness		
To truly understand the *Sermon on the Mount*		
To avoid *dis*satisfaction and cultivate *un*satisfaction		
To constantly learn more about real love		
To savor life's humor		
To achieve self-discovery		
To achieve self-fulfillment		
To achieve self-actualization		
To get a lot done and have a lot of fun		
To always appreciate the value of good sense		
To always appreciate the value of nonsense		

If your dream is not here, please take the time right now to begin to formulate it. *Write it down*. Write it down and carry it around with you. This will begin to add the emotional muscle needed for full expective living.

There is a technique, well known to professional managers, called PERT or *Program Evaluation Review Technique*.

A suggested PERT for expective living appears in Fig. 6.1.

Your expective life plan should be carefully and meticulously developed. It is a way to proclaim your rarity; it is *your own plan*. Note the use of a basic technique that is as old as logical thinking and as modern as now. This technique is built around some doggerel I have paraphrased from Kipling.

> Six true and honest friends have I,
> They give me every clue,
> Their names are what and where and
> When and why and how and who.

They comprise the central muscle for your dreams.

EXPERIENCE IS WHAT WE PERCEIVE

If we cease to expect of ourselves, we cease to be persons. Furthermore, when we cease—or never begin—to expect from others, we literally are detracting from, or denying others their right to full personal growth, full personality, full personhood.

How well I recall a morning years ago when my daughter, Wendy, then thirteen, was competing as an equestrienne jumper at the American Royal, a nationally recognized horse show. We, as a family, were very tense and nervous about this at breakfast. The jumping obstacles were going to be big and difficult, and frankly I was just plain scared about what could happen. I asked Wendy (oh so causally to keep her from sensing my uncertainties), "How do you think you'll do?" She smiled and said quietly, "I've already won. I just haven't told my horse yet." Did she win the blue ribbon? What do you think? No, she didn't but she got second place by five-tenths of a second in a jumpoff between the two riders who had had clear—or no fault—rides earlier.

I believe this illustrates that even though a little girl in her first really big show did not win the first place ribbon, she competed with confidence, skill, and success because of the power of her belief in herself, her horse, and their combined possibilities. I have always thought her statement of expectation was one of the most positive I have ever heard. Contrast this with what probably would have happened if I had ordered, commanded, or directed her to win.

I'll never forget another incident during Wendy's thirteenth year. We were driving along together and as we passed the home of a friend of hers, Wendy commented, "I don't think her dad loves her very much." Her assessment startled me because I happened to think her father was one of the finest, most conscientious, and thoroughly nice guys I knew. In some bewilderment, I said, "What do you mean, he doesn't love her? He talks about her all the time, and he'd do anything for her." Wendy looked at me for a few seconds as though she couldn't understand why I didn't seem to know what she meant. Then, she said something that has had a profound effect on what I—and my colleagues—have subsequently said and taught over much of the world. Here it is. Please think deeply about its significance.

But, Dad, he can't love her very much, because he makes things too easy for her.

How much do *you* love those with whom you live and work?

Do you care enough about them to provide some logically developed obstacles and difficulties—some stretching expectations?

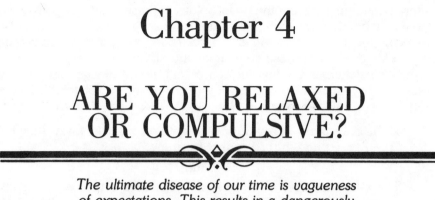

Chapter 4

ARE YOU RELAXED OR COMPULSIVE?

*The ultimate disease of our time is vagueness
of expectations. This results in a dangerously
pallid and drifting nation.*

JOE D. BATTEN

In a recent conversation, my long-time friend and admired compatriot, Dr. G. Herbert True, gave me a most thought-provoking series of statements. They were all on a small card he extracted from his wallet and handed me. I didn't ask who had written it. Perhaps it was Herb. In any event, I'll ask his permission to use it. Here's a warning. It has already changed many lives. Are you ready?

THOU SHALT NOT KILL
Yesterday I killed . . . my son's joy . . . in the victory of his
team. I complained about his dirty clothes—torn at the seam.
The day before I killed my daughter's pride in that dress she'd
made. I pointed out its faults, then added faint praise. One day I
killed a friendship—turned affection to hate. I misunderstood,
that's all—but it was too late. I killed my spouse's love. *Not*
with a mighty blow. It died bit by bit; year by year . . . so slow.
Tonight I saw the light of love die slowly in her look; when she
reached toward me with her hand . . . and I picked up . . . a
book. Oh God of the resurrection . . . take me by the hand.
And teach me how to truly love and loving understand.

PULLED AND STRETCHED

If a typical audience is asked to name the greatest and most successful companies in the world, they will almost invariably mention the IBM and Marriott corporations. In the second half of this book, we will take a much more penetrating look at the philosophies of these great companies. For now let's briefly examine employee relations—how people at work get along and feel about each other. There are some key statements that get at the heart of what these companies are all about.

For instance, in the famous, ten-point Marriott Pledge that is signed anew each year by all managers and supervisors, two statements stand out in the promise each signer makes to the members of his or her team:

To be consistent in my temperament so that they know how to "read" me and what to *expect* from me."

and

To make sure they always know in advance what I *expect* from them in the way of conduct and appreciation on the job.

Please note that the level of morale at Marriott—by all modern indices—is considered unusually high. One can sense this throughout this unusually effective, disciplined, and profitable organization.

IBM is consistently rated by a wide variety of people as probably the most successful company in the world. Its profit is so great that recently when corporate investors were looking for ways to most wisely invest IBM capital, they finally concluded that the best investment was the purchase of IBM stock.

Strange as it may seem, it has been alleged that Thomas Watson, Sr., the founder of IBM, was affected strongly in his early years by Thoreau—the same Thoreau who is often thought of as the "mystic guru of Walden pond" and dismissed by many so-called pragmatic management people as an impractical dreamer, idealist, and poet.

It does not seem so strange when one reflects on some of the quintessential statements of Thoreau who said

You find only the world you look for.

IBM, you see, believes in stretch, not push. It believes in expectations rather than directions. Thomas Watson, Jr., in his thoroughly excellent book, *A Business and Its Beliefs** lists the three basic beliefs that he says were and are at the core of the reasons for IBM's success. Hard on the heels of these three beliefs, which we'll discuss later, is the statement which many feel is the *summum bonum* of the IBM philosophy. It is:

IBM expects and demands superior performance from its people in whatever they do.

---

*Thomas Watson, Jr., 1963, *A Business and Its Beliefs*, McGraw-Hill.

If you have been brainwashed by stereotype, you may have flinched when you read this IBM summation. You may have felt it sounded too severe or arbitrary. The fact is, however, that the morale of people at IBM conclusively shows that when management looks for strengths—for the best in each person and then ensures that they are paid for actual performance—resentments do not simmer. Rather there is a feeling of dignity, worth, and individuality. People feel stretched rather than driven, unleashed rather than repressed, turned on rather than turned off. Strange as it may seem to those brainwashed by many years of permissive and/or abrasive stereotype, it is this "higher road" of expective relationships that speak most squarely to the need for a feeling of *significance* that pervades all of our needs, wants, problems, and actions.

One additional database for the foregoing statements may be perceived in a finding of the American Psychiatric Association. After several years of studying the causes of fatigue in the world today, and most particularly in the United States, they concluded that the *principal* cause of fatigue in the lives of most people is the failure to have something which seems bigger and more important than themselves to live *for*. Stated positively: Having something bigger and more important to live for than ourselves is the finest kind of stretching we can have.

What, then, do *you* conclude is the most fatiguing way to live?

Pulled and stretched?

or

Pushed and pressed?

GROWTH

It is axiomatic to say sagely and wisely that we must grow or perish—expand or atrophy. Let me submit instead that we either *confront our possibilities* or settle for some of our *probabilities*.

Here are some of the most key elements involved.

Goals—vision

Realistic assessment of strengths

Openness

Wonder

Tough-minded expectations

Hope

Goals—Vision

People such as Albert Schweitzer, Carl Jung, Jacques Maritain, Pitirim Sorokin, and others who have left a real imprint on history were goal-oriented. They formulated specific plans to fulfill their vision. Schweitzer, for example, decided at the age of twenty-one that he would consider himself justified in concentrating until he was thirty on science and art in order to devote himself from that time forward "to the direct service of humanity." At twenty-four his first book, on the religious philosophy of Immanuel Kant, was published, and in 1905, at the age of thirty, he took up the study of medicine in order to spend the rest of his life as a doctor in Africa.

Realistic Assessment of Strength

The study of the lives of Lincoln, Churchill, Tolstoi, John Wayne, Andrew Carnegie, W. Clement Stone, Clare Boothe Luce, and literally hundreds of successful people whose backgrounds are widely different and whose achievements cover a broad spectrum reveals one common denominator. They determined what they could do best, set goals, and then *used their strengths*. They had no time to agonize over weaknesses, which are simply the *absence* of strengths.

Openness—Vulnerability

C. S. Lewis in his treatment of love has said that love cannot develop and flourish behind walls of defensiveness. This applies in equal measure to faith, hope, and gratitude as we have discussed earlier. We must be nondefensive, receptive, sensitive, and appreciative in all areas of our life.

Three other powerful values that help comprise the total value of the truly actualized, growing person are truth, goodness, and an appreciation of beauty. These, too, can be perceived, learned, savored, and flourish only in a person who lives with his or her guard down, who stays truly open and vulnerable to people, events, and relationships, indeed, open to the entire world around them.

Wonder

The study of the lives of people such as Lillian Gilbreth, Adela Rogers St. John, Gracie Fields, Abraham Maslow, Marcus Bach, and Maxwell Maltz reveals that they had and have, above all, an abiding *curiosity*. Studies of people in their eighties and beyond reveal that a sense of wonder, of awe about the wonderfulness of the human condition, are common denominators. Recently I had the pleasure of viewing an assortment of these "sprightly oldsters" on television. They included Adela Rogers St. John, author of *Tell No Man* and other great books, who still speaks rapid fire, is still intensely curious, has a new book in process, and one just released. *She is in love with life!* Gracie Fields, pushing ninety, sang a song and exuded sparkle, crackle, and glow. She *laughed a lot.* She has a perpetual sense of wonder! A search for and sensitivity to joy, beauty, and discovery.

Tough-Minded Expectations

Expectations, of course, are the main focus of this book. But what of tough-mindedness? What does it really mean?

It means a resilient, flexible, elastic, open, growing, committed, tenacious, and supple quality of mind. It has nothing in common with hardness, rigidity, abrasiveness, or directiveness. Regardless of one's political persuasion, I believe most will agree that Harry S Truman exemplified tough-mindedness and high expectations during his long, productive, and ebullient life.

Hope

Hope, as we have said, is the universal nourishment of the human being—the central voltage—without which life cannot be maintained for long. With no pun intended, I submit that Bob Hope, the ageless and irrepressible laughmaster, beautifully exemplifies a life of giving, caring, and sharing hope. His life is a testimony to the fact that laughter is one of the great elixirs of Hope.

RECEIVER OR TRANSMITTER?

Marcus Bach, world traveler, perpetual student of the great religions of the world, former chairman of the department of religion in some great universities, author of thirty books, has caught the flavor of what we want to accomplish here in the title of his book *Let Life Be Like This!*

During your life, have you tried in effect to *tell* the world what you want? Do you issue verbal requisitions to people in the form of directive statements? Do you *tell* your colleagues on the job what you want? Do you *tell* your family what you want? Do you *tell* God what you want?

In speeches and seminars over the years, I have suggested that the participants reverse the word "tell" so that it becomes "let." For instance, do you suppose master salespersons became persuasive artists by "telling" people about their products? By making a "pitch"? Salespeople can make a living that way, but they seldom become great. On the contrary, masters of persuasion cultivate strong and visible interests in the wants, needs, and problems of the customer and expresses this interest by

Asking
Listening
Hearing

As they ask, listen, and—above all—*hear,* they let information, insights, and awareness *in.*

As you begin to reflect on and examine the invitation to reverse the "tell" to "let," you may find this to be, initially, an alien thought. Our society has programmed most of us to tell rather than expect. To talk rather than listen. Master salespersons or persuaders often do about 10 percent of the talking and 90 percent of the listening. In this way they "de-fuse and diffuse" the customer's defenses or resentments, help the customer to feel significant, and they *close the sale.*

This is vastly oversimplified. There are literally thousands of nuances, experiments, readjustments, and insights that take place over a period of time as you discuss the sheer pleasure and effectiveness of "reversing the tell."

Let it be like this!

I wonder if you've ever thought of what the world would be like without he's or she's. Pretty grim, of course, and pretty illogical.

Let me close this chapter on a light note.

HE (*H*ope and *E*xpecting) + SHE (*S*ynergy, *H*ope, and *E*xpecting) =

A great future.

Do you agree?

Chapter 5

A SKINFULL OF VARIABLES

There is one thing stronger than all the armies in the world and that is an expectation whose time has come—a magnificent possibility which has become reality.

JOE D. BATTEN

Is there a "science of living"? Can living be a science? I hope not. We humans are not constants, and for the scientific method to apply to us, we would have to be controllable, isolatable, predictable, largely quantitative constants.

We are anything but such quantifiable and predictable creatures. We are "skins full of variables." Every single one of us is significantly different from each other. In fact, second by second, minute by minute, we change greatly from what we *were*. An exciting thought about the future is its sheer unpredictability and variability. Therein lies hope!

THE UNIQUENESS OF YOU

In Francis Thompson's famous poem, "The Hound of Heaven," he describes his flight from God and himself.

> I fled Him, down the nights
> and down the days;
> I fled Him, down the arches
> of the years;
> I fled Him, down the labyrinthine
> ways
> Of my own mind; and in the mist
> of tears

> I hid from Him, and under running
> laughter.
> Up vistaed hopes I sped;
> And shot, precipitated,
> Adown Titanic glooms of chasmed
> fears.

He discovers as the poem unfolds that, while he is, indeed, unique as an individual, he has the same deep spiritual and emotional hungers as everyone else has: A need to love, a need to hope, a need to expect.

Members of a famous psychiatric clinic have been studying the brain tissue of cadavers for many years. Their purpose has been to research the extent to which these people had activated the cells of their brain tissue during their lifetimes. They have found that average persons activated approximately 7 to 8 percent of their total brain cells during their lifetime and that those in the genius category—with accomplishments on the scale of those of an Einstein—activated only some 10 to 12 percent of their brain cells during their lifetimes.

This is, indeed, mind-boggling information. It just begins to illustrate the enormous reservoir of possibilities still sleeping within us. This next statistic may already be dated, but here it is.

The average human brain contains 285,000 times the computative units of the most sophisticated IBM computer.

Needed? Tools to draw out, to evoke, to unfold, to plumb the depths of the human mind. Expectations!

DELIGHTFUL UNPREDICTABILITY

We have seen many determined efforts to organize personal assessment and the evaluation of people into structured techniques. For instance, we consultants and behavioral "scientists" have developed patterned interview and classification forms and records that sometimes miss the whole point of what we should really be trying to ascertain or determine. Please accompany me now on a whimsical and vicarious "interview."

You're a very important executive in a modern, major management organization. It's a beautiful day and you're sitting at your executive work place doing executive things.

The intercom buzzes, your secretary says, "Sir, that executive applicant you were expecting is here." You flip a switch and say in firm, clear executive tones, "Send him in," and resume your executive tasks. The door opens, you get to your feet, raise your gaze and take a good look at the applicant—and—you're shocked.

This man looks *old*, paunchy, homely. His trousers don't match his coat, and he is just not very prepossessing in appearance.

You feel a flash of annoyance because your valuable time is being taken up by this person. But you remind yourself wisely that you must think of company image and give this person the benefit of at least some kind of interview. Besides, here is an opportunity to try out the new and impressive looking "interview guide" that was developed for you by a firm of behavioral scientists. You consult this guide and in clear, executive tones, begin the interview.

"Won't you sit down, sir!" and then you notice he's sitting down. You hastily clear your throat and proceed. "Sir, where did you obtain your business degree?" He responds by saying, "Why, I never received a degree." "No degree?" you say incredulously. "Why not?"

"Oh," he says, "it just didn't seem that important. I studied a lot of things—history, economics, math, philosophy, political science, art. . . ."

"Art?" you interrupt. "You're an executive, and you studied *art?*" "Yes," he says, "I *enjoyed* it; by the way, if you'll study my credentials there, you'll see I've accomplished quite a bit."

"I'm doing the interviewing," you inform him.

Next question: "I see here that you had at one time a serious speech impediment." "Yes," he says, "but that was long ago, and in the meantime I've been described as very fluent and articulate—even eloquent."

"That may be," you say, "but modern behavioral science research indicates that if a person has *ever* had a real speech impediment, for instance, stuttering, like yours, he may lapse back under the stress of fatigue and tension." "Not to worry," he says, "I've actually undergone a lot of stress, strain, and long hours over the years. Will you look at my track record there?"

"All in good time," you say. "Let's establish some other things first." And again you consult the interview guide.

Next question: "Have you ever had trouble within your family? Ever had serious problems with your children?"

"Well, sure, I had some real problems for several years, but they've long since been worked out. Will you take a look there at the results I've gotten on the job?"

"All in good time," you say. "By the way, why aren't you wearing proper executive apparel? Your trousers don't match your coat, and you have cigar ashes on your vest. Is that any way for an executive applicant to dress? It violates executive protocol!"

"I thought you were looking for someone who could get results. I thought you would be hiring my *mind.* The way I dress feels comfortable, and I can *think* better."

By now you feel you have been patient, businesslike, and objective. Above all, you have utilized both the Interview Guide and the Trait Assessment Inventory. You note there is one more question to ask.

"Sir, do you *drink*?" His eyes sparkle and he says, "Yes sir, I *do*." "How much"? *"Two* glasses of brandy *every* evening."

"Every evening?" you ask.

"Yes," he says, "every night." "Do you mean two *shot* glasses," you ask, and he says, "No, two *water* glasses. Incidentally, can we discuss what I've *accomplished*?"

You drop the "diagnostic" instruments in front of you and say. "Sir, I've tried to give you a fair, objective interview. But, I must be honest with you. Here's my assessment."

- You're past our retirement age.
- You do not have the proper educational background.
- You might become inarticulate or incoherent under stress.
- You were unable to adequately manage your family squabbles at key and crucial junctures.
- Your sense of executive protocol and grooming leaves much to be desired.
- The consumption of two tumblers of brandy every night means you are technically an alcoholic.

"I'm sorry, Mr. Churchill, you're not qualified!"

Obviously, the foregoing exercise in facetiousness did not really happen, but I hope to illustrate that when we seek to make people conform to "scientific" or "scientistic" modules, we deny their individuality, significance, and worth. We also lose out on some very productive talent and, incidentally, on a lot of fun.

At Batten, Batten, Hudson & Swab we often seek to explain our proliferating company, and its service by saying

We help people and organizations get a lot done and have a lot of fun. And—you can't do much of one without the other.

At a different and somewhat more profound level, we seek to explain the company in this way.

We are in business to help individuals and organizations become all they can *be*.

STRANGE ENCOUNTERS

Recently I was walking through O'Hare International Airport and some interesting things happened. This particular morning I was walking through the United terminal, swinging my briefcase and kind of bouncing along when I heard a voice. "Hey, Joe, how you doing?" I turned around and walking toward me was a well-groomed, prosperous-looking man. He held out his hand and said, "Joe, it's good to see you. I think I've read almost every book you've ever written." I felt good about that. He went on to say "I think I may have seen all of your films (twenty-one of them). I've heard a lot of your cassettes and, Joe, a while back in Harrisburg I heard you speak for three hours."

I was beginning to glow. I said, "It's really good to see you," and started to walk along. He continued, "Wait a minute, Joe, I'd like to talk to you a little bit. You know, when you think about it, I've spent literally hours in the dark watching you on film and reading those books. I've spent *many hours* of reading, I've even listened to your tapes as I lay in bed."

Well, I decided I should spend a little time with this fellow, so I answered, "That's really interesting." He said, "One of the things that I've gathered from your books is that you believe in candor. There are three different chapters in your books on candor."

I said, "That's right." He said, "You reach a lot of people, don't you?" And I said, "Yes, I suppose I do." He went on, "Well, Joe, I'd like to sit down then and talk with you about *you*. Can we go down to the Red Carpet Room here?" I had about two hours before my TWA flight, so I agreed. As we walked toward the Red Carpet Room, I noticed that this fellow was articulate, intelligent, and sincere. I remarked in a casual way, "What did you want to talk about?" He said, "Joe, like I said, I've really studied you, and I think I have an almost encyclopedic knowledge of your *weaknesses*." Startled, I exclaimed, "What?" paused a moment, and added, "Gosh, I just realize that I'd better get over to TWA and catch my flight."

"When does your flight leave?" he said and, of course, I had to tell him the truth. "No problem," he said, "this'll only take twenty minutes." And so, we continued toward the Red Carpet room.

I found myself walking slightly behind him, hoping I could lose him in the crowd, but he kept an eye on me. When we arrived at the Red Carpet Room, we found an empty corner and sat down for our talk. Sure enough, this was a man of his word; he really had done a job on studying my weaknesses. He proceeded, even though he didn't know he was doing it, to do a job on me. He zeroed right in and, remember, he was articulate, intelligent, and sincere. After about three minutes of this criticism, I felt *bad.*

I sat there knowing that I should be open, that I should *hear* him because I believe in candor. And, yet, in spite of myself, my guard began to go up. The defenses, the retorts, the rebuttal began to form in my mind. I knew I should keep quiet and *listen,* and so I did, but my defenses had risen very high. And, even though I *knew* I should try to hear every word he was saying, I didn't really hear him at all.

Finally, I sensed that the twenty minutes were about over. By then, I had a little knot in my stomach. I didn't feel very well. Even though I didn't know this fellow very well, and he seemed like a nice guy, I had decided there were a few things I should tell *him.*

I sensed that he was about through, and I said, "Yeah, buddy, and I wanted to mention these things to *you* . . ." At this, he jumped up and held his hand out with a big smile and said, "It's been great, Joe. I've got to run." And away he went. I watched him dash out for his plane and muttered after him, "Yeah, buddy, thanks for the dialogue, mostly monologue."

Dialogue, by definition, is "two or more people engaged in monologues," and most of us don't need any more of that.

I sat there with all the starch gone from my spine and a knot in my stomach. Finally, I realized that this would never do. I got up and began to walk toward the TWA area and, as I walked along, I began to sublimate. This means to begin to push a happening to the back of your awareness. As I walked along, I was sublimating. It can be a very healthy defense mechanism.

As I approached the TWA area, I was beginning to feel pretty good again, beginning to get a little bounce back in my stride. As I got within about fifty feet of the boarding area, I heard a voice. "Hey, Joe, how you doing?" I turned around and walking toward me was *another* well-groomed, prosperous-looking guy. He walked up, gave me a warm handshake and said, "Joe, it's good to see you." I said, "Well . . . , it's good to see you, too." But I was not feeling strictly honest about that.

He continued, "Joe, you won't believe this, but I think I've seen *all* of your films." I replied, "That's good. It's . . . good to see you," and started to walk on. He said, "Wait a minute, Joe, would you believe I've read all your books?" As he continued, I thought to myself, "Wow, *another* one"! "And, I've heard a lot of your cassette albums. Joe, you believe in candor don't you?" And I answered, "Well, at the *right time* and *place.*"

He said, "Joe, you reach a lot of people don't you?" And I said, "Well, . . . not as many as you might think." He said, "I know you do, and you are being modest. Joe, I would like you to walk down to the

Ambassador's Lounge with me, I'd like to talk to you for about twenty minutes." I glanced at my watch and saw that I had about an hour left. "I don't know whether I have time or not." He asked, "What time does your plane leave?" And, of course, I had to tell him the truth. He smiled and said, "Plenty of time. This will only take twenty minutes."

I started to walk along with him to the Ambassador's Lounge and, as we walked along, I noticed four things about this fellow. He was intelligent, articulate, sincere, and he meant well. I kind of snapped at him, knowing that I shouldn't, "What do you want to talk about"? He smiled again, "Joe, I want to talk to you about your strengths." Now it was my turn to smile. I would have no need to sublimate this encounter. "Great! Let's talk for a *couple of hours.*" "I'd like to, Joe," he responded, "but I've only got about twenty minutes." "Then, let's get at it," I replied.

Let's recognize what a weakness is. It is the *absence* of a strength! It is a missing thing, a zero, a vacuum, a chasm, a nothing. A weakness is a *nothing!*

This guy zeroed right in on the strengths he had observed and on the additional strengths he felt I have which I haven't even used yet. Even more importantly, he talked about ways I could *use* my present strengths *better.*

My defenses dissolved. I *let him in,* and I *let me out.* The thing called synergy began to happen. If you mix a couple of chemicals together and the result is explosive, it's a synergistic action. When two and two add up to five or more, that is synergy. When the whole is greater than the sum of the parts, that's synergy.

So we sat there and the combined total of two men was significant, because I let him *in,* and I let me *out.* I heard *every* word he was saying and related to his chemistry. I began to think as the minutes went by what a splendid sort of chap this guy was. What a keen judge of character. Obviously, he was an expert at personal assessment, and suddenly I realized with a start that the twenty minutes were almost over. I wanted to point out some of these good things I observed in him and started to say, ". . . yes, and I want to say to you . . .," when he looked at his watch, jumped to his feet, stuck his hand out and said, "Joe, I've got to run; it's been great to see you." And away he went.

Now, remember, over in the Red Carpet Room, when the first man had to dash for his plane, I said, "Thanks for the dialogue—mostly monologue." Now, to this fellow I used a word that *every* reader has heard literally thousands of times. It's one of the most over used and under understood words there is, I refer to the word *communication.* I said, "Thanks buddy, thanks for the communication." Because, you see, that's what really happened.

What is the definition of communication? I have never had any member of a seminar audience who could give me the dictionary definition. And this is one of those instances where the definition of a word actually helps you perceive a lot of things about its meaning, and its anatomy, and how to *do* it.

Here are the four words that define communication.

Shared meaning—shared understanding

These four words, in a sense, say it all. Is there anything more we need for successful relationships? Is there anything more we need for successful family life? for successful job performance?

Let's explore some of the key elements involved in real communication, in real shared meaning and understanding.

This is the reason that I have, albeit somewhat facetiously, chronicled the foregoing composite of hundreds of airport conversations over the years. Here are some of the things that happened in those encounters in O'Hare.

- A discussion of weaknesses usually raises defenses unless one realizes that the only valid reason for identifying weaknesses is to *determine what additional strengths are needed* and/or what is needed to further develop existing strengths.

- When one feels threatened by a weakness-oriented approach, one becomes defensive whether one really wants to or not.

- Only dialogue and monologue can seep through such defenses. Shared *meaning* and shared *understanding* can happen, or take place, only when these defenses are dissolved by a focus on strengths.

- It is very difficult to be open and vulnerable (necessary conditions for real communication) if approached in a weakness-oriented way.

- It is relatively easy to begin to dissolve your defenses and really perceive, feel, and hear what the strength-oriented person is attempting to communicate.

- It is reassuring and reaffirming to learn more about our present and potential strengths. We become able to truly exchange and share intentions, goals, and expectations.

- If we dwell on each other's weaknesses, we'll never truly get to *know* one another.

- If we steadily search for—and *expect* to find—an ever-increasing number of strengths in each other, we can truly come to *know* one another.

As we begin to wind up this discussion of human variables, let's deal briefly with *judgment* and *evaluation*.

The *Bible* tells us that we should not judge others. This causes confusion and concern among many. Thus it has become almost trite to say, "Don't be judgmental."

And yet we must conduct performance appraisals, make many kinds of decisions, and aid our children and others in developing alternatives in their lives and on the job.

It is hoped that the following distinctions and definitions will be useful in addressing this dilemma:

> **Judgment—primarily focuses on weaknesses and is directive.**
>
> **Evaluate —primarily focuses on the strengths and values of the person or event and is expective.**

Judgmental behavior can, indeed, compress, depress, and stultify. Who, indeed, wants to be perceived as an ambulatory skinfull of weaknesses.

Evaluatory behavior can evoke, unfold, expand, and lead. It is an expectant rung on the ladder of hope.

What's your choice?

Chapter 6

BUT—WHAT DO WE DO?

*When we know who and
what we wish to be, we will find
it relatively easy to know what
to do.*

JOE D. BATTEN

Can you live in neutral for a day? an hour? a minute? a second? Researchers tell us that the human body—the human being—just cannot live in neutral at all.

Do we, then, have a choice? Yes! But since that choice cannot be to live in neutral, it boils down to these two options.

We must *build*—with every thought, word, and action—or we must destroy—with every thought, word, and action. Since we cannot live in neutral, there is no in-*between*!

How do we set about designing and creating a life of *building*? A very famous and wealthy man told me that he started each day by sitting on the edge of his bed and mentally reciting the Biblical verse, "This is the day the Lord has made, I will rejoice and be glad in it." This is a very fine thought for flavoring and suffusing each day. What, however, does one do, figuratively speaking, to develop the blueprint, the bricks and mortar, for such construction?

Figure 6.1 lays out a schematic PERT approach and presents a dream, some goals, some skills, and some tasks. This tool should be studied and appropriately adapted to the unique wants and needs of each individual person.

Once you have determined your dream and set out goals, skills, and tasks, you have only stated intentions. It is important to utilize some specifics to enable you to follow through. Table 6.1 illustrates an Action Plan to use for each goal indicated in your dream. Without a plan of

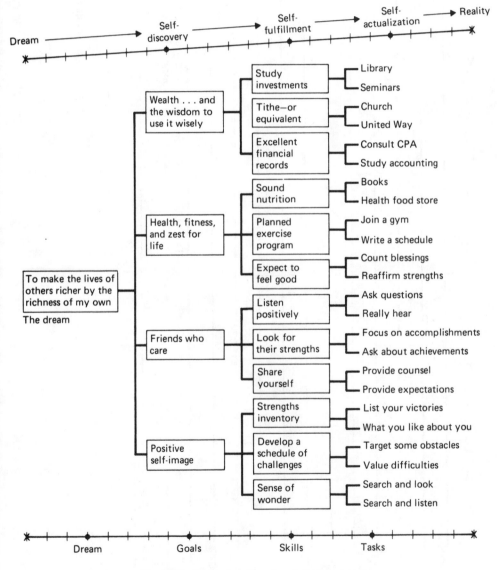

Fig. 6.1 Expective life planning instrument.

Table 6.1 Action plan for expective living.

Major goal _____   Why? _____

Subgoal _____   Why? _____

Action step	Resource requirements (skills, money, training, relationships)	Specific tasks	Target dates	
			Begin	Complete

Table 6.2 Weekly Planning Control Sheet

Specific task	Completed?	Not completed?	(If not completed) Alternative action

action your goals may not mesh into your dream, but scatter and diffuse into nothingness.

Next, it is important to monitor your progress to insure that you are making steady and consistent gains. The Planning Control Sheet in Table 6.2 will help you stay on target and show you are truly getting results.

RESCULPTING LIFE-STYLES

Deep in the mystique of our 200-year-old society is the notion that "a good offense is the best defense." We have all seen this philosophy give impetus to individuals and organizations as they embark on new ventures. However, we have also seen careers, lives, and organizations slow up and plateau long before they should.

What happened? What is needed? Before addressing these questions directly, please reflect on the following.

> **Imagine that last year's football Super Bowl champions, who are ostensibly the greatest football team in the world, came to your town to play your local high school football team.**

> **Can you see it? These huge pros come on the field, averaging about 240 pounds in the line. The backfield studded with former All-Americans. At the other end, warming up, is a group of boys averaging about 180 pounds each and each approximately seventeen years old.**

What would happen? Would the high school team be run over and virtually annihilated?

Actually, the Super Bowl champions could not possibly win—*if* they played nothing but defense. No interceptions, safeties, touchbacks, etc.—*nothing* but defense! If the reader stepped into the ring with the World's Heavyweight Boxing Champion, *he*—the Champion—could not possibly win *if* he did nothing *but* defend.

What I am seeking to bring out here is the sheer and towering futility of basing a whole life-style and strategy around defense. Suppose, as in the case of Bert Farquhar, discussed in Chapter 1, we are successful in insulating ourselves from all dangers, threats, difficulties, and challenge. Suppose, we are able to truly build a "safe" life-style. This implies that we have forged such a ring of defenses around our thoughts, our words, and our *actions,* that we no longer have to discover new strengths, skills, insights, and resourcefulness within ourselves. Indeed, we no longer need to even *maintain* our physical, mental, and spiritual muscle tone. What kind of life would such a safe, well-defended pattern yield? Here are some examples.

- Physical, mental, and spiritual atrophy
- Ultimate lack of real confidence
- Defensive, status quo mannerisms
- Dullness
- A tendency to become petty, vindictive, and self-seeking
- Early obsolescence—at home and at work
- Habits of temporizing and compromising reality
- Become overly directive and aggressive
- Become a receiving set for tensions rather than a transmitter of them
- A tendency to live, talk, and work in terms of what one is *against* instead of what one is *for*
- Habits and mannerisms which *beget* defensiveness from others
- One begins to expect the worst rather than the best
- A tendency to focus on weaknesses rather than strengths
- Growing feelings of insignificance as a human being
- A tendency to become a thermometer (which simply registers the temperature of the climate in which it finds itself) rather than a thermostat (which *changes* the temperature)
- A tendency to covet and savor the purely quantitative elements of life rather than the qualitative
- A tendency to think in terms of negatives such as can't, don't, won't
- A tendency to *destroy* relationships, quality, enthusiasm, and dreams—to become an abominable no-man

I have been blessed with many encounters and experiences that have added to my deep feelings about the sheer practicality, utility, joy, and usefulness of resculpting a lifelong pattern from one of defensiveness to one of vulnerability.

Lillian Gilbreth, that late great lady, is one of the finest examples of vulnerability I have encountered. Here are a few highlights of her remarkable career, which extended beyond her initial role of mother as depicted in the book and movie "Cheaper by the Dozen."

- When her husband, Frank Bunker Gilbreth, died and left her with twelve children to finish raising, she did not spread them among orphanages and relatives (the usual recourse sixty years ago). She took over the small consulting business he had started, made it highly successful, and kept her children together as a family. Each child was able to complete its education.

- She was named the outstanding management thinker in the world and awarded a medal for this in Czechoslovakia.
- She received more honorary degrees than any President of the United States.
- She was voted *Mother of the Year* in the United States.
- She published many influential papers and books on the subject of time and motion study and related areas of work efficiency.

Being aware of these and other achievements of this remarkable lady, I was amazed and delighted to discover on a flight out of Phoenix that she was sitting in the seat next to me. This was some seventeen years ago.

As we began to chat, I asked her a question, something I do whenever I meet a person whose life has been unusually successful. "Dr. Gilbreth, would you mind telling me the secret of your success?" She looked at me with eyes that danced and said, "I'll be happy to tell you. My secret is that every morning I ask the Lord to provide me with some new obstacles and difficulties." And that was it. I was disappointed. I had expected some deep philosophical profundity, I suppose, some learned and abstruse formula or potion for success.

And so, I blurted out, "Is that *it?*" She said, "No, there's more; every night I always *thank* Him because he always *answers* my morning prayer." I was still feeling somewhat puzzled and let down by these answers. They didn't seem to be at all practical and specific in terms of what I had expected from the person who was probably the world's leading authority on efficiency and specificity.

Another effort: "Dr. Gilbreth, you've already told me you're eighty-seven. When do you think you might reach an age when you'll no longer ask the Lord for obstacles and difficulties?" She gave me a big smile and said, "Young man, come around and ask me that when I reach middle age."

She had given me so much, and I had still understood so little. As we flew on toward Denver, she explained the meaning of her brief and sprightly remarks.

> When Frank died, I had some moments of despair and my first thoughts about my family, of course, were for their security. I decided that I just might make a go of the consulting firm and slowly built it toward a satisfying level of profitability. Somewhere along the way I began to realize, as a result of the research I'd carried out, the exciting life Frank and I had had together, and other factors, that boredom and lack of challenge were the chief enemies of a long, happy, and productive life.

> As I steadily evolved toward a practice of actually seeking out challenges and tough situations to research and solve, I came to realize more and more that those were the moments in which I truly felt totally alive, creative, healthy, and happy. I began to notice as the years went by how many of my friends and colleagues lost their health and productive ability in direct proportion to the extent to which they avoided tough and exciting situations. Many of them who played it safe and secure just lost their basic zest for living.

She said much more, but that's the essence of it. She also shared some new research which had recently been conducted among people in their eighties and nineties. Three common denominators were found to be

- They never quit trying to learn more,
- They worked hard,
- They laughed a lot. They had a sense of humor.

Lillian Gilbreth's life was a tremendous testimony to the renewing power of high expectations. She *expected* to find

Challenges	Respect
Difficulties	Growth
Obstacles	Purpose
Confrontation of possibilities	Fulfillment
Feelings of accomplishment and completion	New insights

And, that's what she found!

We have touched only lightly on what I now realize was the most important thing she taught and exemplified. This has to do with a word—a way of life—that is foreign to the macho conditioning of all too many people, particularly men. Here's that word again.

Vulnerability

It requires courage, toughness, tenacity, self-discipline, commitment, and strength to keep your defensive profile low and let life *in* and let you *out*. The most successful men and women I have met on this and other continents are people who might seldom or never actually use the word "vulnerability" but their whole life-style exemplifies

Risk-taking	Anticipation
Openness	Receptivity to innovation and creativity
Spontaneity	

Another encounter: Jerry was a rising manager in a large, animal nutrition organization. He was well educated, hard working, impressive-looking, and on a fast promotional track. However, Jerry was not happy, and he told me he hoped he'd find some answers in the seminar I was presenting to his company in a midwest city. It was just before Christmas and very cold. At the end of the day of seminar, we shared a cab to the airport. When Jerry stuck out his hand to say good-by at the airport, his hand was moist; he appeared under considerable stress and said, "Joe, I'm going to try some of these things you talked about today—just as soon as I get home."

We didn't meet again until three years later in the Texas Panhandle where I was to present another seminar to managers from his company. This time Jerry was the coordinator for the occasion.

At the social hour the night before the seminar, he drew me aside and said, "Joe, I want to share an experience with you that changed my life." "Fire away," I said. Here's his story.

In that seminar three years ago, you said, among other things, that most fathers assumed their kids knew they loved them, but somehow never got around to really *saying* so. I had never really thought about it. I just assumed my daughter knew I loved her because we had a nice standard of living, and she had quite a few nice things. But, you raised a question in my mind. Had I really told her? Did she really know?

I suddenly realized I didn't really know her and decided when I got back home that night, I'd make a point of telling her. On the plane, to my astonishment, I discovered I was actually nervous about looking that thirteen-year-old girl right in the eyes and telling her how I felt.

My nervousness increased as I picked up my car at the airport and headed out for our house in the suburbs. As I walked up to the door, I discovered it was locked, and I didn't have a key.

I pushed on the doorbell and when my daughter came to the door, she opened it carefully and looked rather apprehensively into the darkness outside. As I stepped inside she said in kind of a dull, dutiful voice, "Oh, Hi daddy."

My mind was made up. I suddenly put my arms around her and gave her a big hug. At the same time I said, "I've really missed you and mom and, you know what? I really love you." She had never really remembered me talking like this. As you know I'm not a very emotional-sounding guy and suddenly I felt her go tense all over, and I thought, with a sinking feeling, that

I'd blown it. Then, she suddenly hugged me back very hard, and I heard her murmur, "Daddy, I didn't really think you loved me."

Well, I don't want to go into a long story about the last three years except to say that there was something therapeutic and releasing about what had happened. I really began to work at it, and I found it became easier and easier to feel and express love.

I began to find it easier to build warm and understanding relationships on the job and with customers. But best of all, there were real changes in my family.

The "communication gap" I had felt between both my wife and daughter and me had closed and, Joe, I'm so proud of what that girl is becoming. I guess the thing I'm most happy about is that now I can *tell* her how I feel about what she's becoming and *enjoy* it.

Here was a man who had seemed to have it all and yet the most important parts of his life had been sorely lacking in real meaning and feeling. He had the courage to really do a job of resculpting himself and his life.

DISCOVERING COMMITMENT

Many readers have heard of C. S. Lewis and have read his books. They include such classics as *The Screwtape Letters; The World's Last Night; Out of the Silent Planet; Perelandra; That Hideous Strength; Miracles; The Great Divorce, Mere Christianity; The Four Loves;* and of course the delightful series for children, *The Chronicles of Narnia.*

I'd like to share two major events in the life of C. S. Lewis with you. It is not generally well known that at one time in his life he was an agnostic, virtually an atheist—and a cynical one. He was a philologist, a discipline specializing in the root meanings of words and other symbols of human communication. As a young and superbly trained professor, or don, at Oxford, he set out to debunk the Scriptures and prove that Christianity was a hoax. Armed with the ability to translate Greek and Roman documents and scrolls, as well as other ancient languages, such as Aramaic, the language of Christ, he began a carefully organized program of research. He studied diligently and with great commitment to his "cause."

As he dug deeply into ancient documents, scrolls, parchments, and other ancient works, a strange thing began to happen. He discovered that, instead of documenting and proving the mythical or fictional roots of Christianity, he was experiencing a deep metamorphosis, a profound change in his thinking. The more he researched, the more his newly awakened faith grew. He became one of the best known Christian writers, teachers, and advocates of this century. His writings have influenced the lives of millions of people.

At a later point in his life, he wrote the famous controversial book *The Screwtape Letters.* This book and the movie made from it made C. S. Lewis a financially wealthy man. But, in a strange way which I'll describe, he had become an emotionally and spiritually impoverished person by the time that book was completed.

His own explanation, paraphrased here, tells us what happened.

> **As I worked on *The Screwtape Letters,* I made every effort to put myself in the position of the devil so that as Screwtape wrote to his nephew, Wormwood, he would truly reflect the negativism of the Prince of Darkness. I had to truly think, feel, and write in terms of evil, rot, decay, negativism, and ruin. By the time the letters were finished, my mind was full of itch and scratch and rot. I was literally mentally ill.**

Lewis was, of course, worried and distressed by his condition. Medicine didn't help him. In moments when he emerged from the Slough of Despond, he began to realize what had happened and then to reason that the same methods, in reverse, might enable him to become well.

He had *become* what he *thought*! He had *become* what he *said*!

The only solution seemed to be to *think* and *say* and *write* his way out of the twilight of depression into a condition of mental health and wholeness. Accordingly, he began to write a book entitled *Surprised by Joy.* As he thought and felt and wrote, the dry rot lifted, and he did, indeed, become healthy, vigorous, and optimistic again. His expectations, while initially feeble and halting, grew and were fed by their own achievement.

He became what he *thought*! He became what he *said*! Commitment grows out of expectations. Fulfilled commitments fuel the growth of new and stronger expectations.

FUELING COMMITMENT—CYBERNETICS

What is the stuff of commitment? What are the cybernetics of commitment? Let us be sure first that we understand the basic meaning of cybernetics. It comes from the Greek root word "kybernan" that means "to steer, to govern." Although cybernetic units and servomechanisms are sometimes confused, a cybernetic unit is considerably more than a servomechanism. A servomechanism, as electricians and electronics experts know, is a closed loop wherein energy (electrical in this case) is transmitted and returns to its source via a closed loop and continues to perpetuate and fuel or energize itself. A space vehicle carrying astronauts contains many servomechanisms. The aggregate of all of the servomechanisms add up to total cybernetic unit.

By far the most effective, unique, and sophisticated cybernetic unit contained in a space vehicle is the astronaut, the person. However, human *bodies* are not necessarily human beings. The qualities that enable the human being to make self-correcting choices or *decisions* are the qualities that make him or her truly the most splendid cybernetic unit in our world.

What are these qualities? The capacity to think? No, they are the thoughts generated by the human mind—the *working product* of the mind.

In a speech some years ago at Von Karman Auditorium in Pasadena, I asked the scientists from the Jet Propulsion Laboratory if they could tell me the chemical composition of a thought. Several promptly gave me the chemical composition of *brain tissue*. That, however, did not truly answer the question. Finally, these great scientists (perhaps the greatest group in the world) expressed the belief that a thought really has no chemical composition. As we talked, we agreed that without the mind to express thought, the human body can make nothing practical happen. Our human body is intensely impractical— perhaps ultimately embarrassing—without the mind that promotes it to the status of human *being*.

So, what are some primary kinds of fuel for stoking the cybernetic tanks and control panels we carry around between our ears?

The story of Big Ed may help to provide some insights. I arrived in a city to present a seminar on "Tough-Minded Management" to a group from many kinds of organizations and was met by a group of people who took me out to dinner in order to brief me on the group I would talk to the next day.

The obviously dominant member of the group was Big Ed, a large, burly man with a deep, rumbling voice. At dinner he informed me that he was a troubleshooter for a huge, international organization. His job was to go into certain divisions or subsidiaries to terminate the employment of the executive in charge.

He told me, "Joe, I'm really looking forward to tomorrow because all of these guys need to listen to a tough guy like you. They're gonna find out that my style is the right one." He grinned and winked as he said this.

I smiled. I knew the next day was going to be different from what he was anticipating.

He sat impassively all day long and left at the end of the seminar without saying anything to me.

What I really want to share with you took place three years later when I returned to that city to present another management seminar to approximately the same group. Big Ed was there and at about ten o'clock he suddenly stood up and asked loudly, "Joe, can I say something to these people?" I grinned and said, "Sure, when anybody is as big as you are, Ed, he can say anything he wants." Big Ed went on to say

All you guys know me, and some of you know what's happened to me. I want to share it, however, with all of you. Joe, I think you'll appreciate it by the time I've finished. When I heard you suggest that each of us, in order to become really tough-minded, needed to learn to tell those closest to us that we really loved them, I thought it was a bunch of sentimental garbage. I wondered what in the world that had to do with being tough. You had said toughness is like leather, and hardness is like granite—that the tough mind is open, resilient, disciplined, and tenacious—but I couldn't see what love had to do with it.

That night as I sat across the living room from my wife, your words were still bugging me. What kind of courage would it take to tell my wife I loved her? Couldn't anybody do it? You had also said this should be in the daylight and not in the bedroom. I found myself clearing my throat and starting and then stopping. My wife looked up and asked me what I had said and I answered, "Oh, nothing." Then, suddenly I got up, walked across the room, nervously pushed her newspaper aside and said, "Alice, I love you." For a minute she looked startled. Then tears came to her eyes, and she said softly, "Ed, I love you, too, but this is the first time in twenty-five years you've said it like that."

We talked a while about how love—if there's enough of it—can dissolve all kinds of tensions and suddenly I decided, on the spur of the moment, to call my oldest son in New York. We had never really communicated well.

When I got him on the phone, I blurted out, "Son, you're liable to think I'm drunk, but I'm not. I just thought I'd call you up and tell you I love you." There was a pause at his end and then I heard him say quietly, "Dad, I guess I've known that, but it's sure good to hear. I want you to know I love you, too." We had a good chat and then I called my younger son in San

Francisco. We had been closer. I told him the same thing and this, too, led to a real fine talk like we'd never really had.

As I lay in bed that night thinking, I realized that all of the things you'd talked about that day—real management nuts and bolts—took on extra meaning, and I could get a handle on how to really apply them, *if* I really understood and practiced tough-minded agape love.

I began to read books on the subject. Sure enough, Joe, a lot of great people had a lot to say, and I began to realize the enormous practicality of applied love in my life, both at home and at work.

As some of you guys here know, I really changed the way I approached, worked with, and led people. I began to listen more and to really *hear*. I learned what it was like to try to get to know people's present and potential strengths—rather than dwelling on their weaknesses. I began to discover the real pleasure of helping people build their confidence. Maybe the most important thing of all was that I really began to understand that an excellent way to show love and respect for people was to *expect* them to use their strengths to meet objectives we'd worked out together.

"Joe, this is my way of saying thanks. Incidentally, talk about *practical;* I'm now executive vice-president of the company. OK, you guys, now *listen*."

I hope you will agree that Big Ed was using sound cybernetics. He discovered how to truly strengthen and toughen his mind and then *he reaped what he sowed*! The circle closed and now as he pumps tough-minded love into his life, it returns with compounded interest.

A recurrent theme in this book is that *self-control* is the unique faculty in human beings that characterizes them as fully cybernetic.

A beautiful statement of truth with regard to human cybernetics comes from Tolstoi.

There never has been and never can be a good life without self-control.

Chapter 7

WHAT ARE YOU
PREPARING *FOR?*

*In admitting a new body of evidence, we
instinctively seek to disturb as little
as possible our preexisting stock of ideas.*

WILLIAM JAMES

*The static, fearful mind is,
reposing in a dying person.*

JOE D. BATTEN

*Who can follow a leader who
Simply lives, talks, and works
In terms of what he is* against? *In reality, such a person is
no leader at all.*

JOE D. BATTEN

Do you believe in a life of dissent—or a life of protest? You might say, "Neither one. I want to be a nice person and avoid both." This would premise that the two words are similar when, in reality, they are exactly the opposite.

> **Dissent—To live, talk, and work in terms of what you are *against*. It is from the Latin; meaning "to tear apart from."**

> **Protest—To live, talk, and work in terms of what you are *for*. It is from the Latin; meaning "testament for."**

WE ARE ALL BECOMING—WHAT?

One night in Atlanta, Herb True, Earl Nightingale, and I were speaking at a large rally of several thousand people. Herb spoke first and was, predictably, highly informative, entertaining, and stimulating. I was on next and then I went out into the audience to listen to Earl.

As we all sat there in rapt silence, he shared a distillation of thirty years of experience and research. His central message was that virtually all the great achievements, inventions, fortunes, and unusually productive lives were accomplished by people who went against the tides of their times—people who were anything but "trendy"—people who dared to be different. His examples were many and ranged widely from Jesus Christ and Moses to Thomas Edison. His recurrent theme was that they had dared to go *against* a wide variety of things, people, and circumstances. While I agree completely with the basic sense of what Earl was saying, I would like to propose a radical shift in semantics and please note that the shift is far deeper than semantical per se.

I believe that thousands—perhaps millions—of people have lived lives of dissent over the centuries without the kind of success Earl cited. I believe, further, that it really takes very little courage, discipline, and daring to simply—and I mean *simply—dissent.*

It is, instead, a copout, a way to seek refuge from confrontation and constructive action. The dissenter's vocabulary is full of negatives. He articulates what can't, didn't, wouldn't, won't, etc. happen. Very little courage or mental ability is required to simply live, talk, and work in terms of what you are *against.*

In reality all of those notable examples of success cited by Earl Nightingale were people who had *decided* what to be *for.* Could the American Revolution have succeeded if those early colonists had only decided they were "against" the practices of the British Empire? Rather, an examination of any good American history text reveals that they knew and articulated—through slogans and goals in innumerable ways—what they were *for.* Their expectations seasoned and influenced all that they accomplished.

Did Thomas Edison spend thousands of hours in research and experiments because he was *against* darkness? Or because he was *for* light?

Did Henry Ford invest most of a lifetime in inventing and improving the Ford automobile because he was simply opposed to horses? Or because he was committed to discovering and building a mechanical contrivance that would improve transportation? What he actually said was, "I'll belt the earth with dependable motor cars."

You might find it enjoyable and useful to categorize the following people.

	Dissented?	Protested?
Albert Einstein	_____	_____
Babe Ruth	_____	_____
Norman Vincent Peale	_____	_____
Madame Curie	_____	_____
Robert Fulton	_____	_____
Beethoven	_____	_____
Christ	_____	_____
Moses	_____	_____
Alexander Graham Bell	_____	_____
Pearl Buck	_____	_____
Shakespeare	_____	_____
Plato	_____	_____
Robert Oppenheimer	_____	_____
Aristotle	_____	_____
Socrates	_____	_____
Theodore Roosevelt	_____	_____
Eleanor Roosevelt	_____	_____
Reinhold Niebuhr	_____	_____
Lincoln	_____	_____
Gandhi	_____	_____
Henry Kaiser	_____	_____
Ralph Waldo Emerson	_____	_____
Thomas Watson, Sr.	_____	_____

If you will go to the library and study the lives of these men and women, it will be of inestimable value in helping you supply your own answer to the question

You are becoming—What?

QUALITY OF PURPOSE

We have read earlier the statement by Thoreau: "You find only the world you look *for*." (Italics mine.)

A purpose is an expectation. The dictionary definition of purpose includes

to propose as an aim to oneself

. . . an action in course of execution

something set up as an objective or end to be attained

full of determination

The dictionary definition of quality includes:

a degree of excellence

the character in a logical proposition of being affirmative or negative

superiority in kind

the attribute of an elementary sensation that makes it unlike any other

What quality of purpose do you really *want?* What quality of purpose have you *decided* on?

There is a vast difference between the two preceding questions. Virtually everybody "wants" to live a life of success, excellence, and richness. A relatively small number of people *decide* to live such a life. The power of a purpose, the lift and pull of an expectant dream, cannot be overemphasized.

The following poem was written long before the term cybernetics was part of our vocabulary. It does not sound as sonorous or sophisticated as some of the foregoing definitions, but this might be the place to throw in some mental paprika:

> If you *think* you are beaten, you are.
> If you *think* you dare not, you don't.
> If you *like* to win, but you *think* you can't,
>   It is almost certain you won't.
>
> If you *think* you'll lose, you're lost,
>   For out of the world we find,
>   Success begins with a fellow's will
>   It's all in the *state of mind.*
>
> If you *think* you are outclassed, you are,
>   You've got to think high to rise,
> You've got to be *sure of yourself* before
>   You can even win a prize.
>
> Life's battles don't always go
>   To the stronger or faster man,
> But sooner or later the man who wins
>   Is the man *who thinks he can!*

One of the premier thinkers and writers of several decades ago was Dr. Henry C. Link whose research, thoughts, and writings provided valuable background and foundation for the subsequent work of Abraham Maslow.

Perhaps Link's most significant finding was one that emerged as a product of some research he had been asked to spearhead by a well-funded foundation to determine the principal reason—or common denominator—of happiness in the United States. He assembled a blue-ribbon task force of researchers from various disciplines. They carefully defined happiness and reached unanimous agreement. Then they mapped out a thorough cross section of people for research purposes and began their inquiry.

At the end of a year, they were ready to release a one-thousand-page report to the press. Dr. Link asked the members of the press if they would like a distilled statement that summarized the one thousand pages of data. They indicated they would, indeed, prefer that.

Would you care to attempt to summarize in one sentence just what you feel such a scientific project yielded? Remember the purpose; to determine if there were one or several common denominators in the life of "happy" Americans. Please give it a try.

_____

_____

_____

Here is what Dr. Link found:

Virtually every day of his life, the happy American does, or attempts to do, something *difficult.*

While this was a carefully mapped out scientific study replete with Ph.D.'s of various disciplines, it sounds familiar, indeed, when we review the statements of Dr. Lillian Gilbreth and many others who have been asked to comment.

We *need* to include in our purpose—the quality of our purpose— some tasks which are tough, stretching, and thus a source of discovery, renewal, and happiness.

QUALITY OF RELATIONSHIPS

There are certainly all kinds of relationships: courageous, pusillanimous and cowardly, selfish and greedy, caring and sharing, destructive, synergistically symbiotic, hateful, loving, warm, and cold.

I am submitting here that perhaps the most crucial ingredient in the creating of wholesome, productive and satisfying relationships is courage.

Kierkegaard, Nietzsche, Camus, Sartre and many others have stated in various ways that courage is not the absence of despair; it is rather the capacity to move ahead in *spite of despair.*

Why introduce the idea of despair at this juncture? Because relationships crumble and degenerate into various forms of destructiveness, anger, and negativism when we begin to give up, ever so slightly, on a relationship—a form of despair.

As we examine expectations and possibilities—expective living—it is important to recognize some key elements that induce this kind of despair and some ways to overcome it.

Have you ever been rebuffed or ignored by a sales clerk or a waitress? been snubbed by a maitre d'? paid a huge bill for inadequate work by a plumber? felt the indifference of a doctor, lawyer, teacher, or dentist?

Do you ever find yourself thinking people just don't *care* any more. When that happens, do you feel a small but deep feeling akin to despair?

Why do many people manifest these indications of insufficient caring? I submit that they do it primarily as a defensive reaction to feelings of insignificance which beset them. *Their own self-concept lacks quality.*

Here is an exercise designed to help you gain, regain, or begin to generate a greater feeling of *significance* as a human being.

• Isolate yourself, think deeply, and begin to write down everything you can think of that you expect *from* you. Be sure and do not feel that you are forcing or *directing.* These feelings produce the wrong kind of tensions. Initially you will possibly feel that there are a limited number of expectations involved. Persevere, however, over a number of intervals. Keep seeking, surfacing, pulling, stretching. Recognize that your expectations of you are not limited to *things* but, rather, that they include

Emotions	Growth	Promotions
Feelings	Giving	Building
Reactions	Sharing	Output
Actions	Caring	Input
Relationships	Daring	Vision
Goal seeking	Energy	Awareness
Role seeking	Earnings	

These are only starters. Begin to examine each of the above in terms of What, Where, When, Who, How, and Why

You will begin to experience an unfolding and insightful experience that can add great zest, achievement, and quality to all dimensions of your life.

- The second major step in your development as an expective person is to begin to think and write down what you expect from *others,* particularly those with whom you are in fairly constant association. Here are some starters

Cooperation	Stretch	Forgiveness
Coordination	Affirmation	Compassion
Loyalty	Synergy	Tempo
Candor	Dignity	Empathy
Openess	Laughter	Faith
Vulnerability	Acceptance	Hope
Reinforcement	Sympathy	Love
Counsel	Warmth	Gratitude
Example	Concern	

Again, these are only starters. Begin to examine each of them in terms of

What, Where, When, Who, How, and Why

You'll begin to discover at a gratifying rate that your relationships with others will begin to assume a clarity and a perspective that adds much to the joy of living and working.

- The third major step in the "success continuum" of self-discovery, self-fulfillment, self-actualization is to make a stringent effort to determine what you expect from your own perception of God. The *Bible* will be a great thought-starter here. Depending on your religious persuasion, you can also make excellent use of great religious compendia such as the Koran, the Torah, the Talmudic teachings, etc. Such expectations might include

Truth	Cheerfulness	Self-control
Beauty	Contentment	Patience
Confidence	Courage	Sympathy
Hope	Wisdom	Stability
Happiness	Generosity	Forgiveness
Knowledge		

Once again, these are only starters. Begin to examine each of the above in terms of

What, Where, When, Who, How, and Why

If you care enough, and are disciplined enough, to undertake this expective process, you will find the rewards to be enormous. The *quality of your relationships* will be most rewarding.

THE QUALITY OF YOUR LIFE

Alexis Carrel, the great physician and scientist, spent his lifetime researching and responding to the needs of the human condition. He was curious, committed, and bold in his assumptions about the innate dignity and worth of people. But, more prominent than his boldness was his attitude of hope. Joseph T. Durkin, S. J., wrote

> **The way in which Carrel speculated about the human person was based on an assumption that he never relinquished: Of all earthly beings, man, he believed, possessed a potential for splendor. Man could be intellectually great, his intelligence and capacity for rational intuition were tools. Yet, man need not limit himself to this kind of eminence. He had also the power to amaze the gods with his courage, his kindliness, his moral purity, and his forgetfulness of self for high causes. He could make himself a recorder of deep sensitivity to the most fragile whisper of beauty. He could, in a word, be that very glorious spectacle of a personality in equilibrium with himself and with his environment, and in constant tension toward multiple lofty goals.**
>
> **This was a philosophy of personal excellence surely not useless today. It is, of course, boisterously idealistic. . . . It was wildly idealistic for men to think they could fly, or see and talk to each other across oceans or plant a probe on the moon.***

---

*Specified material from *Hope for Our Time* by Joseph T. Durkin, S. J. Copyright © 1965 by The President and Directors of Georgetown College, Washington, D.C. Reprinted by permission of Harper & Row, Publishers, Inc.

Of course it was idealistic. Can anything truly practical happen without ideals? An ideal is an expectation of possibility. It is the nourishment of practical achievement. Our ideals comprise the thermostat that determines and regulates the quality of our lives.

What are *your* ideals? What are you *for?*

Chapter 8

THE ULTIMATE PRACTICALITY

I have come that you might have life, and have it more abundantly.

THE CHRIST

Do you dare to open yourself to the riches within you?

JOE D. BATTEN

There is some sense and much nonsense thought and spoken with regard to practicality. Note, in fact, the variation within the definition of the word practical from Roget's *Thesaurus*.

workaday, useful, applied (*Use*)

businesslike, orderly, systematic (*Business*)

realistic, unromantic, down-to-earth (*Reality*)

worldly, sophisticated, cosmopolitan (*Experience, Wisdom*)

For instance, the notion is widely held that anything truly practical must be a "hands on" kind of thing. You must be able to see or touch it. What nonsense!

Please think deeply about these questions:

- Can the human *body* function as a human *being* without the mind?
- Can the body and mind create a blueprint or put a nut on a bolt or operate a vacuum cleaner or assemble and launch a space craft without thought?
- Is there any chemical composition to a thought?
- Can a practice-able (practical) thought achieve anything until it is translated into an idea?
- Will ideas flourish and be consistently put into practice without expectancy and hope?
- Can you really *do* anything significant until you know what to *be*?

HOPE + QUALITY + EXPECTATIONS = POSSIBILITIES

To further indicate the practicality of all that has been said so far, in this book, permit me to share some thoughts with you about three separate kinds of examples from widely disparate frames of reference. They are

Vince Lombardi

Konosuke Matsushita

Some great leaders of history

Coach Lombardi was a phenomenon in the world of sports, notably football. In just a few years he had coached the Green Bay Packers up from perennial losers to Super Bowl Champions. Now they had won the Super Bowl twice in two years, a feat that was unparalleled in football.

The television commentator asked Lombardi an excellent question—pithy and succinct. "Coach, what's the secret of the success of the Green Bay Packers?"

Lombardi didn't hesitate a moment. He flashed those big teeth in a smile and said, "These guys love each other." And the interview was over. In the ensuing years, I have asked literally hundreds of times in seminars if anybody remembered that brief and beautiful question and answer. Few do, and it is too bad because Lombardi was not being facetious or dramatic. He meant exactly what he said. The true secret of the success of a team that was, according to experts, older, smaller, and slower than any other major professional football team was exactly as he said.

Coach Lombardi had labored mightily to help his players understand that expecting the best of each other *on and off* field was the best possible indicator of real respect, real love. In this way he helped, and expected, them to care enough to

- Reach and maintain top physical and mental fitness
- Contribute to the loyalty and synergy of the team
- Compete with themselves
- Continue growing as total individuals
- Become individual leaders
- Build a high measure of self-respect
- Look for, and relate to, the *strengths* of each other
- Feel part of a goal greater than self

Two favorite terms of Coach Lombardi were synergistic symbiosis and mental toughness. He knew that the toughest-minded emotion of all, agape love, was the most crucial ingredient.

Many people around the world have heard of the fabulously successful Matsushita Industries, headquartered in Tokyo. It is frequently cited as one of the most successful companies in the world.

In a letter to me, Mr. Matsushita distilled the reasons for his success, a success made more notable by the fact that the company had to start up from scratch after World War II. Thus it is much younger than most other great companies around the world. Here are some statements which Mr. Matsushita considered to be at the heart of the company's success:

> **There are many secrets of success, but the most important one, I think, is *looking at people's strong points* and an attitude of making the most of them.**

> **I think it is better to look at each other's strong points and try to develop them.**

> **Even if I noticed their defects, if they had more strong points, I asked them to do the job.**

> **We have to try to recognize their good qualities and work with them.**

> **If instead I had only noticed their weak points and worried that I did not like their character, I would not have been able to ask anyone to work for me. There would then have been *no working together*.**

It is so illuminating, and eminently practical, to examine the actions and techniques of some of the great leaders of history. From Caesar to Jesus Christ, from Moses to Alexander the Great, we perceive an expective, evocative pattern of *leading*—not driving.

- They led by example and *asked* much from their followers.
- They knew involvement must precede commitment if it is to be pursued with conviction.
- They expected much and made no promises of ease, wealth, and comfort.

Contemplate if you will the short, powerful leadership expective uttered by Christ:

Follow me!

Now we arrive at the heart of expective living. I proffer one more expective profundity:

> **You can develop wise and practical answers only after you have determined the questions.**

Earlier I pointed out that the three great expectives that loom out of the Bible comprise the acronym ASK.

Ask and it will be given you.

Seek and you will find.

Knock and it will open unto you.

Please notice that each of these statements is cybernetic, each is a duality, each has expectation and reward, each is an expective and a result.

Will you do it?

Fig. 8.1 The cybernetic circle of expective living.

1. Know what you can and will expect from you.

2. Let yourself perceive all of your possibilities.

3. Determine specific components of your dream.

4. Decide on the what, where, when, who, how, and why of what you want to *be* and *do*.

5. Determine *how well* the goals can and must be realized.

6. Schedule, prioritize, develop your "life calendar."

7. Apply your mind and skills diligently.

8. Believe in you, in others, and in God. Believe others are right unless proven wrong.

9. Believe in your expectations.

10. Love is the central source of energy that makes it all happen.

11. The highest form of mental and spiritual health.

12. Let life *in*. Seek, quest, appreciate, enjoy.

13. Dissolve your emotional defenses.

14. Savor the flavor of each passing *now*.

15. A sure guarantee of growth, change, and fulfillment.

16. Perhaps this is the finest way to *express* all of the other portions of the circle.

Part II

EXPECTIVE MANAGEMENT

Of course, we need love and respect from others,
but we won't feel fully *significant* about ourselves
unless our "conscience" tells us we are employing,
using, and constructively *realizing* our possibilities.
High expectations, expressed in sound mind-stretching
objectives, speak to those deep needs and help us
fuse and focus our human resources.*

*Joe D. Batten, 1978, *Tough-minded management*, Amacom.

Chapter 9

THE EXPECTIVE PHILOSOPHY

THE CALF PATH
(Traditional Strategy)

One day through the primeval wood
a calf walked home as good calves should;
but made a trail all bent askew,
a crooked trail as calves all do.
Since then three hundred years have fled,
and I infer the calf is dead.
But still he left behind his trail,
and thereby hangs my moral tale.
The trail was taken up next day
by a lone dog that passed that way;
and then a wise bellwether sheep
pursued the trail o'er vale and steep
and drew the flock behind him, too
as good bellwethers always do.
And from that day, o'er hill and glade,
through these old woods a path was made.
And many men wound in and out,
and dodged and turned and bent about,
and uttered words of righteous wrath
because 'twas such a crooked path;
but still they followed . . . do not laugh,
the first migrations of that calf.
This forest path became a lane,
that bent and turned and turned again.
This crooked lane became a road,
where many a poor horse with his load
toiled on beneath the burning sun
and traveled some three miles in one.
And thus a century and a half
they trod the footsteps of that calf.

The years passed on in swiftness fleet;
the road became a village street;
and this, before men were aware,
a city's crowded thoroughfare.
And soon the central street was this
of a renowned metropolis,
and men two centuries and a half
trod in the footsteps of that calf.
A hundred thousand men were led
by one calf near three centuries dead.
They follow, still, his crooked way
and lose one thousand years a day,
for men are prone to go it blind
along the calf paths of the mind
and work away from sun to sun
to do what other men have done.
They follow in the beaten track
and out and in, and forth and back,
and still their devious course pursue,
to keep the path that others do.
They keep the path a sacred groove
along which all their lives they move.
But how the wise old wood gods laugh
who saw the first primeval calf!

AUTHOR UNKNOWN

Somehow the phrase, concept, and aggregate of procedures known as "Management by Objectives" or "MBO" has never gone into the kind of orbit of success that was expected when it surfaced and was first articulated in the fifties.

Business, government, academic, social, and religious organizations have experimented with Management by Objectives with varying degrees of success. Many have perceived it purely as a mechanism, a proliferation of papers, forms, and control dates—all too often as a purely quantitative "exercise" in management. In other instances it has taken on the dimension of a cure-all, potion, panacea, magic formula, etc. This latter premise seems to hold that once you have "set" objectives, no other action is necessary or that the job of *accomplishing* the objectives is 50 percent done. Others have seen it as "a program of MBO," a staff or management tool, rather than a pervasive organizational *way of life*, a pervasive *system*.

In most instances where MBO has yielded less than the desired payload, common denominators such as the following are found.

- Insufficient research, most particularly the need to determine "What exactly is our business; what can and do we do *best?*"
- Insufficient involvement and participation in the formative stages by the people concerned.
- Conceived, taught, and installed as a "managemental program" rather than as a "managerial system."
- No perceived connection between MBO and motivation.
- Insufficient provision for people, feelings, emotions, values: ergo, failure to connect with *reality.*
- No real identification with the "program" by the people involved.
- MBO perceived as a coercive or directive tool rather than as an evocative, expective system.
- MBO perceived as a subsystem to coexist with other organizational systems rather than an overall system that integrates other systems.
- The exclusion of qualitative objectives.
- Failure to understand that if MBO is to truly speak to the needs of the organization, it cannot be "statically organizational" but rather "flexibly organismic."
- Failure to integrate personal goals with company goals. The technical elements of MBO exist only on paper. *People* make it happen.
- Failure to perceive its intrinsic team building capacity.

Enough of this focus on what hasn't, couldn't, shouldn't, didn't, etc. happen! What is needed?

We begin by examining the definition of the word *objective* by Webster and Roget.

> Objective — mission; object; end; purpose; goal; something toward which effort is directed; a strategic position to be attained or purpose to be achieved by a military, operation; a lens or system of lenses that forms an image of an object.

Anything in these definitions that excites you? Does the word objective turn anyone on? How can we build an exciting, unusual, and highly productive system on a foundation that is just plain unexciting by definition?

On the contrary, how do you feel when you read words like the following by Daniel Burnham?

> Make no little plans; they have no magic to stir men's blood and probably themselves will not be realized. Make big plans;

aim high in hope and work, remembering that a noble, logical diagram once recorded will never die, but long after we are gone will be a living thing asserting itself with ever growing insistency.

Or these words by Dr. Alexis Carrel:

Men grow when inspired by a high purpose, when contemplating vast horizons. The sacrifice of oneself is not very difficult for one burning with the passion for a great adventure.

Or these words by William Ellery Channing (1780-1842):

I call that mind free which is not passively framed by outward circumstances, which is not swept away by the torrent of events, which is not the creature of accidental impulse, but which bends events to its own improvement, and acts from an inward spring, from immutable principles which it has deliberately espoused.

It is for precisely these reasons that a carefully worked out philosophy is needed to guide and fuel the entire management system of an organization. The right kind of guiding philosophy has been proven time and again to be the most practical single step an organization can take toward success. The philosophy of an organization should provide

Vision—a grand design

Identification

Stretch—a quickening of the pulse

Integration of the values of the organization

Motives

Spirit

Positivism

Hope

Harry Emerson Fosdick said, "No life ever grows great until it is focused, dedicated, disciplined." I will paraphrase that here, "No *organization* ever grows great until it is focused, dedicated, disciplined."

ASKING IS CARING

What are your responses to the following questions?   YES NO

•   Does every person in your organization fully understand his or her expectations of the organization and of himself?   ____ ____

- Does every manager in your organization fully understand his or her expectations of the organization and of himself or herself? ___ ___

- Does the chief operating officer in your organization fully understand his or her expectations of the organization and of himself or herself? ___ ___

- Does the Chief Executive Officer fully understand his expectations of the organization and of himself or herself? ___ ___

- Do *you* fully understand what you expect from the organization and from yourself? ___ ___

Can we, in *reality*, truly build an organization that is focused, dedicated, and disciplined until such a system of expectations is determined, clarified, and communicated. *Is there anything more practical?* I think not, because the fulfillment of expectations is the only reason for the existence of our organization, our jobs, and everything we say, think, do, and are.

I hope it is noticeable throughout this book that many questions are asked. This is by design because I believe that questions are infinitely more powerful than declarative statements. Do you agree?

Can you think of any really important pervasive even in your life that was consummated by a declarative statement? For instance, I know of no proposal of marriage (that was successfully consummated) that was issued in the form of a command. Do you?

Questions—strong, caring, expective questions—can be very firm and virtually always achieve more real results than directive or declarative statements. It does, however, require real work and real behavioral change to be able to do this because more attention will need to be given to timing, place, mood, facts, circumstances, and individual wants, needs, and problems.

A philosophy of asking, listening, caring, and really *hearing* has been indivisibly associated with highly successful people over the centuries.

Do you care enough?

IBM AND MARRIOTT

A national survey conducted by *Money* magazine indicates conclusively that "IBM is the best company to work for in the United States." Procter and Gamble, Xerox, and Eastman Kodak are close behind. Then we find in the following order: 3M, General Electric, Weyerhaeuser, Cummins Engine, DuPont, J. C. Penny, Mobil Oil, General Foods, and Citicorp. According to the article, what sets these companies apart and makes their employees enthusiastic and loyal is a general commitment to excellence and a sensitivity to human problems.

What is the secret of IBM? Let's read the following quotes from *A Business and Its Beliefs* (1963, McGraw-Hill) by Thomas Watson, Jr.

> Consider any great organization—one that has lasted over the years—and I think you will find that it owes its resiliency not to its form of organization or administrative skills but to the power of what we call *beliefs* and the appeal these beliefs have for its people.
>
> This, then, is my thesis: I firmly believe that any organization, in order to survive and achieve success, must have a sound set of beliefs on which it premises all its policies and actions. Next, I believe that the most important single factor in corporate success is faithful adherence to those beliefs.
>
> And finally, I believe that if an organization is to meet the challenges of a changing world, it must be prepared to change everything about itself except those beliefs as it moves through corporate life.
>
> In other words, the basic philosophy, spirit, and drive of an organization have far more to do with its relative achievements than do technological or economic resources, organizational structure, innovation, and timing. All these things weigh heavily in success. But they are, I think, transcended by how strongly the people in the organization believe in its basic precepts and how faithfully they carry them out.

These basic beliefs are three in number. They are simple, tough, and expective. In each instance, I'll list them along with Thomas Watson, Jr.'s commentary.

> I want to begin with what I think is the most important: *Our respect for the individual.* This is a simple concept, but in IBM it occupies a major portion of management time. We devote more effort to it than anything else.

This basic belief was articulated many years ago and was ahead of its time. IBM recognized that before you can respect others and thus really lead or manage or sell or persuade others, you must possess the confidence that can come only from *self*-respect. Accordingly, their policies, procedures, and practices were geared to accomplish this through training programs, enriched work assignments, interpersonal relationships, and general managerial emphasis.

. . . it also is a succinct expression of our second basic corporate belief. *We want to give the best customer service of any company in the world.*

It has been said by people from smaller companies that this is well and good for an international giant to say, but it probably would not apply to them. In actuality, this expectation was expressed *before* IBM became a giant. It is, rather, one of the major *reasons* it became a giant.

Everybody connected directly and indirectly (this included marketing, quality control, engineering, manufacturing, and other elements of IBM) recognize that this is a broad, generic, but very real, performance standard that undergirds the specific standards in their individual jobs. It is a clear, stimulating, and omnipresent expectation.

The third IBM belief is really the force that makes the other two effective. *We believe that an organization should pursue all tasks with the idea that they can be accomplished in a superior fashion.* **IBM expects and demands superior performance from its people in whatever they do.**

May I add one more quote from Mr. Watson here? It beautifully illustrates the power of clear and high expectations.

Believing in success can help to make it true . . . we constantly acted as though we were much bigger, much more sophisticated, much more successful than any current balance sheet might bear out.

The power of belief transmitted into expectations—this is the story of IBM. I am amused when people tell me that their conceptions of IBM is one of lockstep conformity, even rigidity. This simply does not stand up under scrutiny. I recall, in Atlantic City, spending a day of seminar with assorted executive development officials from IBM's operations from all around the world. They were anything but conformists! Never have I spent a day with a more creative, freewheeling, innovative, and challenging group. They came expecting much, and this is the most crucial element in any stimulating situation. Moreover, it is my experience that *all* IBM employees know these basic beliefs.

IBM is not great because of random chance or happenstance. The company has built and forged its success through a system of expective management virtually unparalleled in the world today.

Although the Marriott Corporation was not listed among the top ten in the study by *Money* magazine, it is difficult to determine why it wasn't. Certainly, by virtually all indices of success, it is truly exemplary.

It was my great privilege and pleasure to speak to all of the Marriott managers at the Marriott Twin Bridges Hotel in Washington, D.C., in

1972. The evidence of high morale, commitment, and loyalty was almost a tangible force and as I listened to and viewed the presentations of key executives with regard to annual achievements and projections, I knew that this was certainly one of the great organizations.

At lunch on the second day of this meeting, I had the pleasure of getting further acquainted with Bill Marriott, Sr., and Bill Marriott, Jr., who had recently become president. I asked them to tell me the secret of the success of Marriott that had been started in an A&W Root Beer shop by Bill Marriott, Sr., and his wife during the 1930s. The senior Marriott smiled and said it was because they practiced the ten elements of the Marriott Pledge. I thought this seemed a bit oversimplified and turned to Bill, Jr., with the same question. He, too, smiled and said that was certainly the single most important factor.

He went on to say that performance standards, performance appraisals, compensation reviews, promotions and all key administrative decisions and perquisites had to be demonstrably based on the Pledge. I asked for a copy and have since taught these expective principles many times.

Each year every member of management of Marriott receives a copy of this pledge and again signs it and sends it back to headquarters where it goes into his personnel file. Here it is in toto.

MARRIOTT CORPORATION

January 17, 1972

TO: Myself

SUBJECT: A Pledge for 1972; A rededication to Excellence in Leadership.

I promise the members of my team
1. To set the right example for them by my own actions in all things.

2. To be consistent in my temperament so that they know how to "read" me and what to expect from me.

3. To be fair, impartial, and consistent in matters relating to work rules, discipline, and reward.

4. To show a sincere, personal interest in them as individuals without becoming overly "familiar."

5. To seek their counsel on matters that affect their jobs and to be guided as much as possible by their judgment.

6. To allow them as much individuality as possible in the way their jobs are performed, as long as the quality of the end result is not compromised.

7. To make sure they always know in advance what I ex-pect from them in the way of conduct and performance on the job.

8. To be appreciative of their efforts and generous in praise of their accomplishments.

9. To use every opportunity to teach them how to do their jobs better and to help themselves advance in skill level and responsibility.

10. To show them that I can "do" as well as "manage" by pitching in to work beside them when my help is needed.

Signed _____

Please note that each one of these statements is really a philosophy in itself. If the average manager decided to take any one of these and really study it and utilize all of its possibilities, the sheer practicality—the changed attitude, manner, and style—would be convincing indeed.

For instance, notice the commitment and self-discipline required in the first statement above. ". . . in *all* things." In the seventh promise, or expectation, note the commitment here to really thinking the job through, planning well in advance, prioritizing needs, and requirements and a willingness to be evaluated.

Certainly, this entire pragmatic pledge illustrates the here and now applicability of the great cybernetic promise:

By their fruits ye shall know them.

Or, paraphrased for today's manager

By your fruits (*example and results*) they will know you.

A CAUSE BIGGER THAN SELF

It's time to take a close look at the differences in meaning and potential applications thereof, of the words *objective* and *expective*.

Objective—**The very definition of the term connotes a lack of feeling. It sounds inanimate, mechanical, and static. It does not sound dynamic, renewing, or motive-actional. It connotes a polar point. It is the opposite of subjective, and humans are intrinsically subjective.**

> Expective—This suggests anticipation, fulfillment, expansion, change, and growth. It provides for expression and accomplishment of feelings. Whereas an objective represents attainment, or some degree of attainment, an expective represents fulfillment or some degree of fulfillment.

From the great leaders of history to modern times, masters of motivation have known that the most important single factor in motivation, particularly when basic subsistence needs have been met, is commitment to a cause greater than self—commitment to an achievement which transcends purely material consideration.

The course of nations, of societies, have changed when the basic ideas of their leaders changed. In business, for instance, General Motors was profoundly influenced by the introduction of new and broad strategic ideas by Alfred Sloan. The Ford Motor Company began an evolution to modern management concepts with Robert McNamara and Lee Iacocca.

The so-called practical manager who ignores the potential of ideas does an injustice to his or her organization.

Please ponder the power of applied thought. It is the essence of practicality.

When the Mahatma Gandhi was asked how he proposed to lead India, the fifth largest nation on earth, to freedom from the might of Great Britain, he grinned and replied, "With love and truth."

IT WORKED!

Chapter 10

THE
EXPECTIVE STRATEGY

*To know what is clearly expected
of one is to tap the wellsprings
of true motivation.*

JOE D. BATTEN

Our major concern here is to highlight the following expective principle.

Strategy should create an attitude of mind focused on tomorrow's expectations and opportunities rather than on yesterday's mistakes and failure.

Next, it should provide an enlightened and unifying foundation for expectations and action plans.

THE OVERALL SYSTEM

Figure 10.1 illustrates the macrocosmic view of expective management. A brief overview follows.

Research— **Take a searching look at all discernible information concerning where we are now and what we need and expect to accomplish.**

Plan— **Clarify, analyze, evaluate, and synthesize the key elements needed to achieve our overall expectations.**

Organize— **The synthesis that emerges from the planning phase determines the type of organization needed to fulfill our planning expectations.**

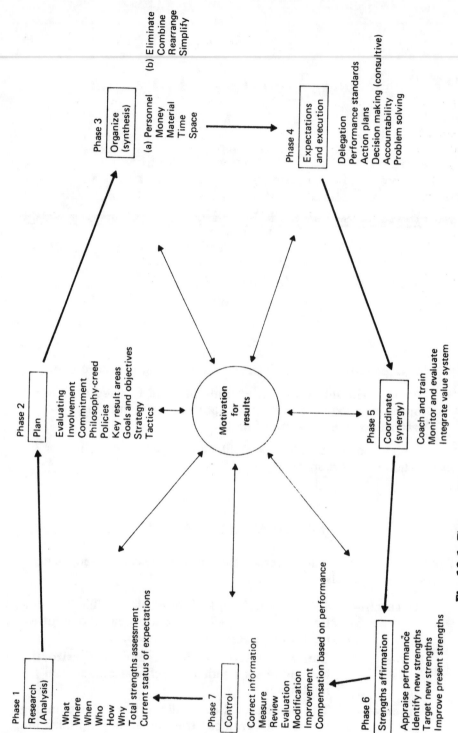

Fig. 10.1 The overall expective management system (Management by Expectations).

Expectations
and
execution—   Here we are moving from *managemental techniques   to   managerial   practices*—systematic
practices needed to implement ongoing and day-
to-day operations.

Coordinate—   Take steps to ensure blending and meshing of
talents, skills, intent, and technique to achieve a
whole that is greater than the sum of the parts
(synergy).

Strengths
affirmation—   This, on a continuing and never ceasing basis, is
perhaps the most crucial commitment of all
since strengths are the *only* tools any person or
organization possesses.

Control—   Our management information system must provide, at clearly targeted intervals, the information needed to know whether we are on target
or otherwise.

The loop closes, and we have the basic schema for a cybernetic
system of expective management.

A CONCEPTUAL VIEW

Figure 10.2 is designed as, it is hoped, a stimulating (albeit sketchy) and
somewhat different approach to the anatomy of an organization. A
relatively unique step is the addition of an organizational element to
provide for possibility thinking. Possibilities that may be lurking in all key
result areas should be constantly under study and experimentation. I
cannot overemphasize the importance of this attitude and practice.
Strangely enough, it is seldom currently done by most organizations.
When the experienced management consultant assesses the temperature
and climate of an organization, he or she can readily detect the symptoms of a lack of possibility thinking.
Some of these symptoms are

No clearly programmed flow of new products or services

Static policies, procedures, and practices—out of date

Key people not trained in the latest techniques

General confusion

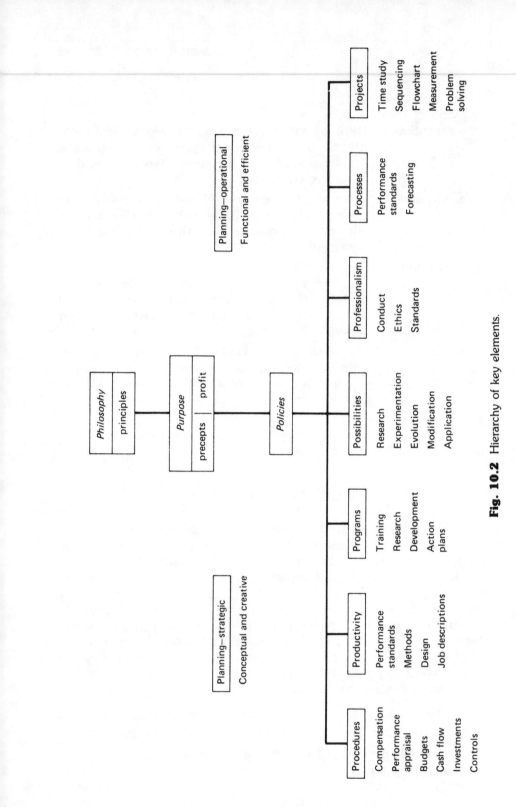

Fig. 10.2 Hierarchy of key elements.

Inconsistent decision making
Poor coordination
Inconsistent controls

WHEN is the best time and place to optimally deal with the needs of our people? _____

_____

WHO is outstanding? Who needs improvement? Who is having difficulty communicating with whom?

_____

_____

HOW can we improve interpersonal skills, construction of internal media (house organs, bulletin boards, memos, meetings, etc.) and other methods of communication?_____

_____

WHY do we believe that true communication (shared meaning— shared understanding) is the very heartbeat of excellent management? _____

_____

THE EXPECTIVE MANAGEMENT SYSTEM—OPERATIONS

Robert Randolph, creator of Planagement, has described strategy as *determining* the right things to do and tactics as *doing* things right. Figure 10.3 is designed to provide a meld of both strategic and tactical steps— an expectancy-fulfilling prophecy and procedure.

Figure 10.3 illustrates a total sequential approach to effective management. Before discussing each of these sixteen steps, let us study a comprehensive set of changes that help prepare for expective management, that help it work, and that are indicators that excellence in management has become and/or is becoming a reality.

These changes include

From	*To*
Pushing	Leading
Expects the worst	Expects the best
"Importance"	Significance
Insecurity	Positive fulfillment

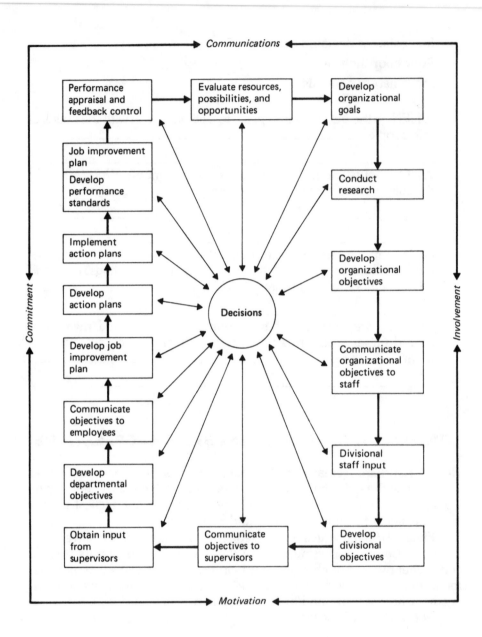

Putting It All Together!

Fig. 10.3 Expective management—operations.

From	*To*
Programs	Systems
Compromising expectations	Clear, stretching expectations
Defensiveness	Open, warm, thoughtful candor
Activity documents and reports	Performance progress reports
Hunch and guess	Disciplined decisions
Inconsistency	Consistency
Conformance	Individuality
Competing with others	Competing with self
Complexity	Simplicity
Avoidance of problems and needs	Confrontation of problems and needs
Dialogue	Real communication
Crises and fire fighting	"Early warning systems"
Office politics	Team synergy
Blurred, expedient morality	Tough, stretching moral climate
Reaction to symptoms	Action dealing with cause
Disparate, dissonant actions	Unity
Compensation based on actions, personal characteristics	Compensation based on positive performance
Fragmentation and diffusion of effort	Purpose and direction
Getting	Giving
Preoccupation with weaknesses	Optimizing strengths (the only tools we possess)
Commitment to self only	Commitment to goals and objectives that transcend self
Benign neglect	Caring
Negative listening	Positive listening
Dis-satisfaction (past-oriented)	Un-satisfaction (future-oriented)
Dissent	Protest
"Gamesmanship"	Accountability for results

From	*To*
Superficial preoccupation with behavioral science jargon and patois	Analysis, evaluation, synthesis and synergy of possibilities
"Affirmative Action" jargon and "dialogue"	Evaluating all people on the basis of performance

Let's examine some of the implications and requirements of each step:

- *Evaluate resources, possibilities, and opportunities*
Less than forty years ago, business and most other kinds of organizations could largely ignore external conditioning factors and, to a lesser extent, internal conditioning factors that now must be considered in all sound strategic and tactical planning. Today we perceive the frightening omnipresence of daily change and ferment of myriad governmental, social, economic, political, and religious factors as well as the sheer volatility of the human condition.

Does any executive dare ignore these conditioning factors? The executive does so at his or her peril. Externally we must consider the global ramifications of the energy challenges, inflation, crises in confidence affecting government leaders; changing consumers' demands based upon things like the alleged new morality; the seeming escalation of the "junk food mentality"; a desire for quick, expedient solutions to all kinds of problems; the drug scene and a host of other symptoms of restless groping throughout the planet, the tough-minded effective manager expects to base organizational strategy on a keen, rational assessment of these factors

> *What* are the expectations of your customers, publics, or constituency? Do you know? It is crucial to find out.
> *Where* do they expect their needs to be met? Where do you expect to fulfill them?
> *Who* is your market? Do you *really* know?
> Have you truly assessed consumer motivations and expectations?
> *How* should these constituencies be best served? Have you mobilized the best data and ideas from your staff?
> *Why* are you in business? Do you actually know precisely the basic utility you are ostensibly organized to serve? What is it?
> *When*—at what clearly targeted intervals—will the above questions be addressed and resolved?

As we consider internal conditioning factors, we are principally concerned with attitudes and all that connotes. What do you, the manager, expect? If you encounter a staff member in the shop, factory, office, or elsewhere, and he or she asks:

"What do you expect from me?" Do you know?
"What do you expect from your job?" Do you know?
"What do you expect from the future?" Do you know?
"What are your general and specific expectations?"

• Do you know how to answer the staff member?

On the other hand, if you ask one of your key people the same questions, will they know?

Do you see what we are saying here? The following managemental tools and managerial considerations must all derive from, and be directly shaped by, the clarity and relevance of mutual expectations.

Performance standards	Accountability
Goals and objectives	Responsibility
Action plans	Authority
Policies	Job descriptions
Procedures	Action improvement plans
Programs	Analyses
Possibilities	Studies
Processes	Organizational structure
Practices	Compensation administration
Performance appraisals	Communication and
Decision making	motivation techniques
Delegation	

To repeat:

All of these key components of effective management do indeed derive from, and are directly shaped by, the clarity and relevance of the expectations from top to bottom and side to side throughout the organization.

• *Develop organizational goals*
Once a sound expective philosophy has been formulated, we are ready to proceed with goals. Although the nomenclature of management terms and sequence varies within organizations, we are suggesting here that goals be considered as broader, more general, and more timeless than objectives. Goals represent transitional expecta-

tions from philosophy to objectives and are frequently expressed in terms of five years or more. I am suggesting that on balance, the chief executive officer's primary accountability is for *strategic* planning (conceptual and creative) and the chief operating officer's primary accountability is for *operational* planning (functional and efficient). For instance, the chief executive officer might indicate clearly what he or she is expecting in terms of organizational goals in the following key result areas. (His or her expectations should be strongly influenced by the research findings in phase one.)

Profitability
Market position
Innovation
Productivity
Physical resources
Financial resources

Manager performance and development
Worker performance and attitude
Public responsibility
Spirit of the organization

- *Conduct research*
Here the chief operating officer or counterpart assumes the direct responsibility and accountability for developing specific objectives to accomplish and fulfill the expectations flowing from the philosophy, research, findings, and goals of the organization. Further specific research is needed then in order to formulate statements of expectation that meet the following definition.

> *An objective is a specific statement of quality, quantity, and time values.*

Objectives (expective) will begin to emerge and become specific and quantified when the five W's and an H are applied to the key result areas above.

- *Develop organizational objectives*
This subject has all too often been treated as arcane, mysterious, and complex. Let's see if we can cast it in a relatively simple mold.

Function	*Key events*	*Objectives*
Production or	Determine key results areas	Clear, concise statements of what is to be accomplished by when. Should be both quantitative and qualitative.
Marketing or		
Administration or	Obtain goals	
Engineering or	Input by subordinates	
Finance or		

Function	Key events
Industrial relations or	Draft rough objective statements
Other key or divisional functions	Select most significant statements
	Discuss, review, evaluate
	Adjust or modify
	Develop action plans
	Coordinate with superior
	Discuss and negotiate
	Agree on modifications
	Proceed with action plans
	Feedback and discussion with team
	Establish feedback and controls

- You may find it useful to review Figs. 10.4 and 10.5.
- *Communicate organizational objectives to staff*
Here is one place in which we deviate significantly from the current practices of most organizations. All too often, the members of the management team and those at lower organizational levels do not have an opportunity to truly participate in the information-gathering phase of the formulation of these management instruments. In expective management, the process of communicating the new goals and objectives to the staff is a highlight. It is significant and stimulating to all employees—not just to the management staff— *because,* as we studied internal conditioning factors in phase one, we carried out the following.

1. Ask *every* employee to submit the following expectations.
  a) Benefits

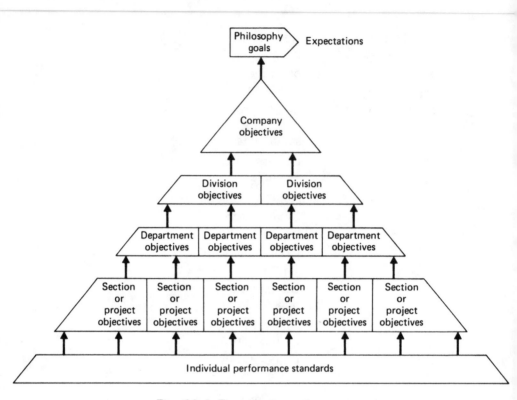

Fig. 10.4 The objective-setting process.

b) Work standards
c) What the organization should become
d) Products, services, innovation
e) Methods improvement
f) What the company should expect from *them*
g) Facilities and working conditions
h) Morale factors

2. They were given these requests in the most simple and succinct forms possible and strongly encouraged to complete and return these expectations.

This may sound complex, time consuming, and expensive. And some organizations probably should not do this for various reasons. The benefits, however, are many and practical.

1. Employees feel significant, listened to, valued as individuals.
2. They feel they "had a hand" in something bigger than themselves.
3. They feel some emotional investment in "their plan."

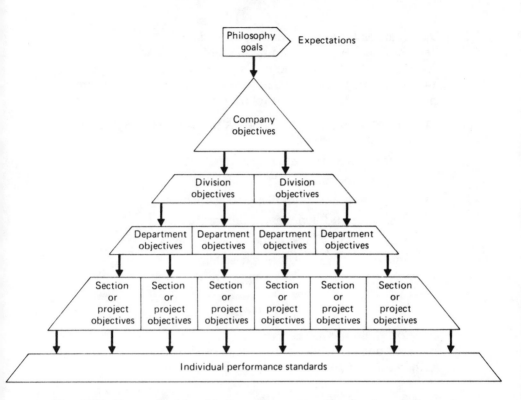

Fig. 10.5 The result of the objective-setting process (the direction of effort and energy).

4. They have enhanced feelings of belonging, opportunity, security, and recognition.

5. Very importantly, they will expend more energy, *work harder and smarter* to meet and fulfill the new expectations.

It is worthwhile to take the time, ideally with the use of video techniques, and carefully choose the place, to fully explain the whole rationale to the staff.

However, I am getting ahead of our sequence. We are still communicating the tentatively formulated objectives to our immediate staff. It is important to listen to them and *hear*. Be sure, too, that you ask penetrating questions to determine precisely why they feel as they do. Finally, it is crucial that you, the boss, remain in an open and vulnerable posture. If you are directive, brusque, or defensive, forget it! You will only be carrying out a charade.

Ask
Listen
Hear

- *Divisional or team input and cooperation*
  Be sure you have obtained agreement well in advance concerning the form, format, and time factors involved in obtaining staff input. It is important that your team interact with you in a way that helps ensure the presence of the following.

  1. Understanding, consonance, mutuality, and agreement concerning the objective(s)
  2. Shared meaning—shared understanding
  3. Respect and trust
  4. Supportive and reinforcing relationships
  5. Resolving and synergizing differences
  6. A perception of the value of team play
  7. Shared and synthesized expectations

  Ask
  Listen
  Hear

- *Develop divisional objectives*
  Here, essentially, we can use the steps shown in Fig. 10.4 and add further sophistications as desired. For instance

  Eliminate
  Combine
  Rearrange
  Simplify
  Synthesize
  Synergize

- **Eliminate —** Scrutinize all categories of data and intent with the idea of removing any work, action, or expectation that will not discernibly contribute to organizational objectives, goals, or philosophy.

  Combine — Extract those key elements that may blend for a leaner, cleaner, and more meaningful statement of expectation.

  Rearrange — To ensure the best blending and meshing of all elements of the objective.

  Simplify — Can any obscure or befogging words, phrases, or sentences be cleaned up for clarity and perception?

> Synthesize — Are the objectives developed and worded in such a manner that their synthesis adds up to synergy? Will two and two equal five or more? Is the whole greater than the sum of the parts?

- As each divisional manager presents his or her objectives, it is important that he or she be expected to fully provide the *Why* of each statement.

The expective manager is curious, disciplined, analytical, and caring.

- *Communicate objectives to supervisors*
Perhaps we should pause here to ensure that the objectives or expectives do, indeed, meet our requirements. Some crucial questions should be asked at each organizational stage or level concurrent with the development of the objectives at that level:

1. Is the objective well written?
   a) Is it specific?
   b) Is it short range with a targeted completion date?
   c) Does it state a result—a specific expectation—rather than an activity?
   d) Are the results measurable?

2. Is the objective one you should pursue?
   a) Is it profit-oriented?
   b) Is it stretching?
   c) Is it attainable?
   d) Is it quantifiable? qualifiable?
   e) Is it practical?
   f) Is it important?
   g) Will it contribute to the objectives of the next higher level and in turn to the organization's objectives. (See Figs. 10.4 and 10.5.)

- *Obtain input from supervisors*
Throughout this chapter I have sought to emphasize that it is crucial to involve your people in the formulation of all objectives. This is equally important for objectives for which they are directly accountable and overall organization objectives to which their component objectives contribute. Table 10.1 supplies some guidelines for implementing this phase.

Table 10.1 Plan for Getting People Involved in Departmental Objectives

	Target dates	
	Begin	*Complete*
• Review and discuss company and division objectives with department.	_____	_____
• Meet with staff to discuss key result areas.	_____	_____
• Write tentative objectives.	_____	_____
• Review tentative objectives with division manager.	_____	_____
• Review and discuss tentative objectives with staff. Make necessary or appropriate changes. Assign research projects necessary to develop specific figures for objectives.	_____	_____
• Write final department objectives.	_____	_____
• Review final objectives with division manager.	_____	_____
• Review and discuss final objectives with staff. Obtain their agreement and commitment.	_____	_____
• Review final objectives with the department. Obtain their agreement and commitment.	_____	_____
• Submit final objectives to division manager for approval.	_____	_____
• Modify objectives as necessary.	_____	_____
• Distribute department objectives to the department.	_____	_____

This procedure illustrates the more formal aspects of the involvement that took place in the development of the department objectives. It does not illustrate the many informal meetings and discussions with individual members of the staff and the department.

- *Develop departmental objectives*
- *Communicate objectives to employees*
  The guidelines in Table 10.1 apply equally to phases 10 and 11.
- *Develop job improvement plan*
  For almost two decades we have heard of attempts to improve the design of jobs. First came "job enlargement" and then "job enrichment." I feel that the product of these efforts has been largely ineffective because of the directive influences pervading the concept.

What Is Needed?

Company expectations thoroughly and comprehensively clarified. Divisional expectations thoroughly and comprehensively clarified. Departmental expectations thoroughly and comprehensively clarified.

Sectional expectations thoroughly and comprehensively clarified.

Individual and personal expectations thoroughly and comprehensively clarified.

With this sound basis of expectations as bedrock for really effective and motivated effort, we can create jobs with stretch, reality, and relevance.

Sir Winston Churchill said:

I pass with relief from the tossing sea of Cause and Theory to the firm ground of Result and Fact.

How can we be more practical than to commence job improvement with a comprehensive understanding of the expectations of the organization as a whole, the specific work unit, and the individuals involved? Does this call for the abolishment of corporate sections or departments that exist to write job and position descriptions? Definitely not! It simply suggests a different method of accumulating the data for the position description. Please remember that, while a *wish* is often only a euphemism—half felt, half thought through—an *expectation* is something you have *decided* you want to give or get, build or destroy, share, confront, and *accomplish*.

Within the organization it must, of course, be understood that the employer's expectations are primary. They have priority. The employer provides compensation, financial and otherwise, and has every right to expect that his or her expectations will be met. It is eminently practical, however, to eliminate guesswork so that the following self-defeating phrases are not felt or heard:

That's not *really* what I wanted to do.

That's not *really* what I want out of life.

I don't *really* understand why I'm expected to do that.

Doesn't the company know what it wants?

My job isn't what I thought it would be.

Nobody knows what's expected around here.

I know what I'm *told* to do, but it doesn't make sense to me.

I don't really like what I'm doing.

I see no relationship between my job and what I'd expected.

And this serious one.

I don't know what they really expect; I just know what I'm *told* to do.

One more plaintive one.

They never ask me what I want and expect.

As you might well imagine, there are a thousand variations of these laments. A well-defined job should be the product of analyses which include the following.

What should be done. What is expected.

Where it should be done.

When it should be done.

Who is expected to do what, where, and with whom.

How expectations are to be fulfilled.

DEVELOP ACTION PLANS

We will elaborate on this important phase in the next chapter and, accordingly, will give it short shrift here.

Even though we might construct the entire system model shown in Fig. 10.3, but exclude the provision for action plans, it wouldn't really fly. Just as a mechanically and electronically sound rocket might be constructed, placed on the launching pad, and filled with fuel, nothing significant would happen unless the actual firing mechanism were activated, the "button pushed."

So it is with the action plan. Fine- and appropriate-sounding statements of philosophy, goals, and objectives will just "be there" unless there is a particularized, nuts-and-bolts, how-to-do-it subassembly to activate it.

DEVELOP PERFORMANCE STANDARDS

If management goals are the outgrowth or product of the organizational philosophy, if objectives are the outgrowth or product of management goals; if action plans are the outgrowth or product of management objectives; and if performance standards are the outgrowth or product of action plans, then it is axiomatic that standards of performance are, indeed, crucial to modern effective, expective management.

What, precisely, are performance standards? First, an objective is something you want to get *done*. Thus a standard of performance *describes the conditions* that will exist *when a job is well done*. Let's pursue this further and examine some other definitions.

A performance standard is a statement of conditions that exist when a job is satisfactorily done.

It is a statement of what constitutes adequate work.

It is a written statement of conditions that will exist when a job is being well done.

. . . standards of performance say *how well,* rather than *what.*

To illustrate the variety of "standards": "How much should I sell" is called a quota; "How much should I measure" is called a "specification"; "How much should I spend" is called a "budget"; and "When should I deliver" is called a "schedule."

The central point in the context of this book, however, is that the performance standards are *all expectations.* Many documents we have seen in client companies called performance standards per se are misleading since they are often gradations or levels of expectations. For instance, a lean, clean format we favor is illustrated in Table 10.2 where "standard" is shown as the indicator of "adequacy." Meeting the next higher "goal" is an intermediate level of performance leading to "excellence" with its proportionately higher rewards. This provides for simplicity, clarity, and stretch.

On the other hand, please note the detailed definition and comprehensive standards in Table 10.3. This, too, is a fine example of clarity and precision albeit much longer. Table 10.4 illustrates a succinct, meaty format.

The key question is: Does it give the particular organization what it needs to meet its expectations? Again, we suggest the following tools of analysis:

Eliminate—What, Where, When, Who, How, and Why

Combine—What, Where, When, Who, How, and Why

Rearrange—What, Where, When, Who, How, and Why

Synthesize—What, Where, When, Who, How, and Why

Synergize—What, Where, When, Who, How, and Why

Some of the outstanding organizations that have committed time and resources to developing standards of performance are

The Boeing Company

Continental Can Company, Inc.

Detroit Edison Company

Diamond Alkali Company

General Electric Company

General Foods Corporation

General Time Corporation

International Business Machines Corporation

Lever Brothers Company

Table 10.2 Sample Performance Standards Format

Performance standards for _____

Objective	Standard	Weight	Goal	Weight	Excellence	Weight
		30%		45%		50%
		6%		8%		11%
		1%		2%		5%
		1%		2%		5%
		2%		4%		6%
		2%		3%		4%

Performance standards for _____
Page two

Objective	Standard	Weight	Goal	Weight	Excellence	Weight
		1%		2%		3%
		2%		3%		5%
		5%		6%		11%
Total		50%		75%		100%

_____ President's signature   _____ Date

Table 10.3 The Western Company standard practice instructions and position guide*

POSITION TITLE: Secretary–treasurer and manager of finance
ACCOUNTABLE TO: President
BROAD FUNCTION:
The secretary–treasurer and manager of finance is accountable to the president for successful and efficient conduct of all finance and accounting functions and for the required financing of the company. Is responsible for providing advice and counsel on company financial matters. Is responsible for the successful and profitable conduct of data service operations.

Is responsible to the president, board of directors, stockholders, and courts for detecting, notifying, and following up to see that proper action is taken so as to prevent fraud, embezzlement, misappropriation of funds, and the like.

Within company policies the secretary–treasurer is responsible for and has commensurate authority and accountability for:

1. Development and recommendation of financial policies.
2. Performing all financial functions of the company, including accounting, budget compilation, internal auditing, reporting, banking, safekeeping, office services, cash receipts, and disbursements, credit and collections, accounting methods and statistics, financing, insurance, and payrolls.
3. Serving as secretary for the company.
4. Serving as treasurer for the company.

PRINCIPAL RESPONSIBILITIES

A. Secretary

1. Maintains minutes books of corporation and issues certified copies of resolutions as appropriate.
2. Attends board of directors' meetings and stockholders' meetings, and records minutes of the proceedings.
3. Signs and attests certificates, statements, and reports.
4. Issues notices of board of directors' and stockholders' meetings.
5. Makes arrangements for meetings of the board of directors and stockholders.
6. Is liaison with attorneys.
7. Is liaison with statutory state agents.
8. Maintains stockholders list.
9. Accepts service of process.

*Reprinted, by permission of the publisher, from *Objectives and Standards: An Approach to Planning and Control,* Research Study 74, Ernest C. Miller, © 1966 by American Management Associations, pp. 83–86. All rights reserved.

Table 10.3 Continued

B.   Treasurer

1. Banking relations: Recommends depositories for company funds. Maintains cooperative relations with personnel of banks and other financial institutions.

Measures for Accountability	Standard
a) Quality of recommendation	a) Approved
b) Number of complaints	b) Number
c) Confidence in treasurer	c) Line of credit and interest rates

2. Capital expenditures: Approves release of funds when available for capital expenditures.

Measure for Accountability	Standard
Action taken	Yes or no

3. Cash flow: Formulates disbursement procedures for accounts payable, payrolls, and the like.

Measure for Accountability	Standard
Takes maximum discounts with lowest bank balance while maintaining satisfactory credit with suppliers	Percent of discounts taken

4. Contracts: Reviews contracts for financial, tax, and risk considerations when requested.

Measure for Accountability	Standard
Problems as result of inadequate review	Number

5. Custody
   a)   Acts as custodian of funds of the company.

Measure for Accountability	Standard
Valuables secure	Approved system for security and losses

   b)   Acts as custodian of securities, notes, mortgages, patents, contracts, insurance policies, or other such documents.

Measure for Accountability	Standard
Important contract documents centrally located and secure	Approved system for security and losses

   c)   Establishes surety bond requirements.

Measure for Accountability	Standard
Action taken	Losses

Table 10.3 Continued

6. Investment: Recommends the most advantageous use, including timing, of the company's cash resources.

Measure for Accountability	Standard
Percent of cash invested	Return on investment

7. Financial control
   a) Recommends action to maintain equity position and working ratios in the long-term best interests of the company.

Measure for Accountability	Standard
Written recommendation	Approved

   b) Plans future cash and financing requirements.

Measure for Accountability	Standard
Written recommendation	Approved

8. Financing
   a) Arranges for needed short-term borrowing.

Measure for Accountability	Standard
Action taken	Terms

   b) Arranges long-term loans.

Measure for Accountability	Standard
Action taken	Approved

   c) Formulates and negotiates details of capital financing transactions.

Measure for Accountability	Standard
Action taken	Terms

9. Insurance: Determines and administers insurance program covering all assets and risks.

Measure for Accountability	Standard	
Completeness and cost of coverage; program in balance	a)	Approved by president
	b)	Number of uninsured losses compared with saved premium
	c)	Loss ratio of those items and appraisal of the risk and service cost
	d)	Ratio of uninsured losses to cost to insure

Table 10.3 Continued

10. Real estate
  a) Purchases, sells, and leases property as instructed.

Measure for Accountability	Standard
Action taken	Yes or no

  b) Negotiates, approves, and pays real estate and personal property taxes and assessments.

Measure for Accountability	Standard
Action taken	Yes or no

11. Signature
  a) Signs checks.

Measure of Accountability	Standard
Action taken	Yes or no

  b) Signs and cosigns contracts, stock certificates, and other such documents.

Measure for Accountability	Standard
Action taken	Yes or no

12. Taxes
  a) Detects effect of tax changes on the company's operations.

Measure for Accountability	Standard
Promptness of detection of changes	No added cost through lack of anticipating effect

  b) Keeps responsible positions informed and takes appropriate action to minimize taxes.

Measures for Accountability	Standard
1. Action taken	1. Yes or no
2. Minimum taxes	2. Dollars

  c) Develops and recommends most advantageous use, including timing, of changes in laws and regulations.

Measure for Accountability	Standard
When minimum taxes are paid	Tax trends

Radio Corporation of America
Standard Oil Company of California
Xerox Corporation

The sequential steps are much the same as those involved for creating and establishing all key steps in Fig. 10.3.

Table 10.4 Whirlpool Corporation's plant manager's standards of performance

| Job responsibility | Standard | Performance | | | Work plans and remarks |
		First quarter	Second quarter	First six months	
1. Maintain efficiency in the work force to a level of	97%	97.2%	98%	97.6%	Continue developing the full-day work concept with hourly employees.
2. Operate to a quality index level of	70%	82%	89%	85%	Work on process one for continued improvement.
3. Control perishable tools per work hour so it does not exceed	18¢ per work-hour	18¢	17.5¢	17.75¢	Work with tool engineers for continued tool life improvement.
4. Control scrap percentage of the direct labor dollars earned so it does not exceed	.095%	.08%	.07%	.075%	Continue present program.
5. Control factory supplies per work hour so it does not exceed	9¢ per work-hour	8.5¢	8¢	8.25¢	Continue present program.
6. Maintain variables as budgeted: First quarter Second quarter First six months	$43,153 $35,820 $78,973	$45,477	$28,480	$73,957	Second six months' goal: $74,025. Continue scheduling programs to achieve new goal.
7. Control unscheduled overtime so as not to exceed	$84.00 per week	$87.50	$86.50	$87.00	Establish more frequent scheduling meetings.
8. Control lost hours so as not to exceed	$325.00	$245.00	$105.00	$175.00	Plan to average better than goal.
9. Maintain safety standards to the extent of no lost-time accidents and a reasonable amount of medicals		11 medicals, no lost time	10 medicals, no lost time	21 medicals, no lost time	Continue to emphasize safety to exceed 1 million work-hours without lost-time accident.
10. Maintain a housekeeping at the level of	100%	99%	99.5%	99.25%	Continue present emphasis.
11. Attain a cost reduction goal of	$55,301	$12,508 (26% attained)	$62,490 (113% attained)	$74,998 (139% attained)	Through May, revised goal: $145,691.

Key result area

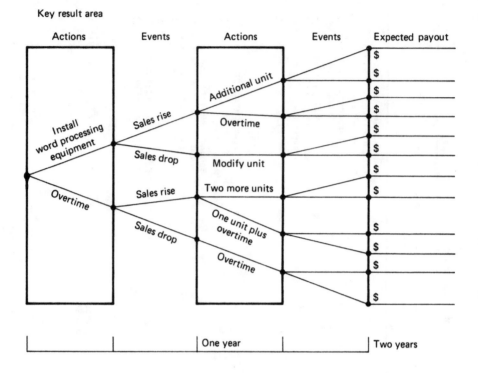

| Actions | Events | Actions | Events | Expected payout |

Fig. 10.6 Expective strategy model—decision making.

If standards have been directly "set" by the superior officer without adequate *involvement* there will not be adequate *commitment*—practiced with *conviction*.

To review:

- Make sure the *Why* of performance standards is thoroughly explained.
- Provide adequate instruction concerning form, format, and procedure.
- Agree upon control dates for submission of preliminary drafts, necessary discussion and counsel, and final draft.
- Try to ensure that the agreed upon standards are lean, clean, fully relevant, and—above all—understood by your team members.

A sample follows.

Setting Performance Standards

Performance standards:

_____

_____

_____

_____

Criteria:

1. Is it specific?
2. Does it state an end result?
3. Is it measurable?
4. Does it have a targeted attainment date?
5. Is it practical?
6. Is it attainable?

Here is an actual example of one of the performance standards of a plant manager:

> **Establish a new quality control program as a fundamental part of manufacturing thinking and action that will contribute substantially to customer satisfaction.**

Evaluate this standard using the previous criteria.

_____

_____

_____

_____

How would you rewrite it?

_____

_____

_____

_____

Evaluate each of the following examples in the same way. If the performance standard can be improved upon, write it!

1. Increase overall typing speed and reduce errors on all finished memos and reports.
    OK?___
    Should be rewritten as follows: _____

    _____

    _____

    _____

2. Reduce total department overtime premium incurrence from $5,000 to $3,000 during the next fiscal year.
    OK?___
    Should be rewritten as follows: _____

    _____

    _____

    _____

3. Achieve further substantial improvement in manufacturing quality, delivery time, and cost reduction by December 31, 19__.
    OK?___
    Should be rewritten as follows: _____

    _____

    _____

4. Enforce safety code to reduce overall production line accidents by January 1, 19__.
    OK?___
    Should be rewritten as follows: _____

    _____

    _____

5. Improve the skills within the finance department through participation by finance personnel in outside seminars, workshops, and plant visits.
    OK? ___
    Should be rewritten as follows: _____

    _____

    _____

Chapter 11

THE EXPECTIVE ACTION PLAN AND PERFORMANCE APPRAISAL SYSTEM

And now . . . let us build muscle into our dreams

JOE D. BATTEN

What is an action plan? What should and can we *expect* from an action plan? We can show its expected role in the general scheme of things thusly:

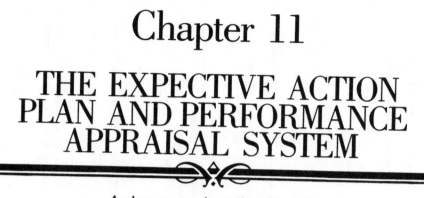

Definition and determination Phases

Implementive Phase

Define wants, needs, and problems
↓
Formulate a philosophy
↓
Formulate and define goals
↓
Formulate and define key result areas
↓
Formulate and define objectives
↓
Formulate and define performance standards

Action plan = Expectations

In Table 11.1 we see one kind of action plan. This is only an updated variant of the kind of thing that began when cave dwellers sketched out the objects of their hunt on cave walls and then carved out the spears or crude weapons with which they would achieve the result.

The first generally known technique that was systematic and relatively sophisticated was the well-known Gantt Chart that chronologized the projected events and affixed dates and things to be done. Since then, we have seen the advent of Critical Path Methods (CPM) and Program Evaluation Review Techniques (PERT).

Table 11.1 Expective management action plan

KRA _____

Major objective (expective) _____

Subobjective (expective) _____

Action step	Resource Requirements (people, money, materials, relationships)	Progress Events	Method of Measurement	Time Control					
				Begin		Complete			PAYOUT EXPECTED
				Earliest	Latest	Earliest	Latest		

PERFORMANCE, APPRAISAL, FEEDBACK AND CONTROL

These techniques have been practiced for at least two decades and have been very useful in organizations in which a multitude of disparate units must come together to form an operating whole (an automobile) or a single functional structure (a building). Both Critical Path Methods and PERT have greatly increased the efficiency of innumerable enterprises and overall operations.

Recently, managers have been expected to construct their own individual action plans to achieve committed objectives. Such individualized action plans provide clarity of sequence and are useful in coordination and feedback. If such a plan is properly coordinated and discussed until there is mutual agreement with one's organizational superior, it tends to further ensure understanding, cooperation, and synergy. We no longer need hear wan and futile statements such as

But I didn't know you'd need that much space.

Didn't you understand how many people I'd need?

I thought *you* were going to . . . .

***Now* you tell me it's not in the budget.**

If we'd only gotten our heads together, this wouldn't have happened

Ad infinitum

CONSULTIVE DECISION MAKING

The modern expective manager is tough-minded. He or she understands Theory Y and the meaningful and usable substance of behavioral science findings.

He or she believes in and practices consultive decision making. That is, he or she does the following.

1. Provides excellent training and example for team members.

They know the what, where, when, who, how, and why of their jobs and the organization.

2. Expects "completed staff work."

a) Subordinates do not bring the manager problems. Rather, they do the research, thinking, and preparation for which they are paid and then present the manager with appropriate proposals or recommendations. In this way he or she can truly "manage by expectation and exception" and make full use of the skills for which *he* or *she* is paid. The manager is in a position to reject, modify, or ratify the proposal. (See Fig. 10.6)

3. Listens carefully, solicits the best input and suggestions from appropriate subordinates and only makes the decision if it is appropriate for the subordinate to do so.

4. Makes the decision if he or she *should* with the full awareness of his or her accountability for its success.

5. Strives always to push decisions down to the level where they should most properly be made. The manager strives to back the decisions of his or her subordinates firmly, consistently, and fairly. The manager expects this of himself or herself, and he or she expects his or her members to provide the same type of support to him or her.

6. In short, prior to making major decisions, the manager strives to utilize the wisdom and resources available to him or her and those subordinate to him or her and then he or she:

Asks
Listens
Hears

Decisions are what the manager is paid for! Are *you* a consultive decision maker?

PERFORMANCE APPRAISAL AND FEEDBACK CONTROL

Today perhaps the most discussed management "tool" in the country—even in the world—is performance appraisal.

And yet, it is not a tool. It is an *aggregate* of tools and, properly meshed, it is a valid subsystem that is an integral part of the entire expective management system.

The following fourteen phases (Fig. 11.1) will describe the key expectations that comprise this subsystem. For our purposes here we will treat it as a modular system.

Phase 1: Philosophy, goals, and objectives of the organization

These key macrocosmic elements are, of course, the full and complete reason for the existence of performance appraisals. Such appraisals are carried out to increase the growth and skill and thus the *positive perfor-*

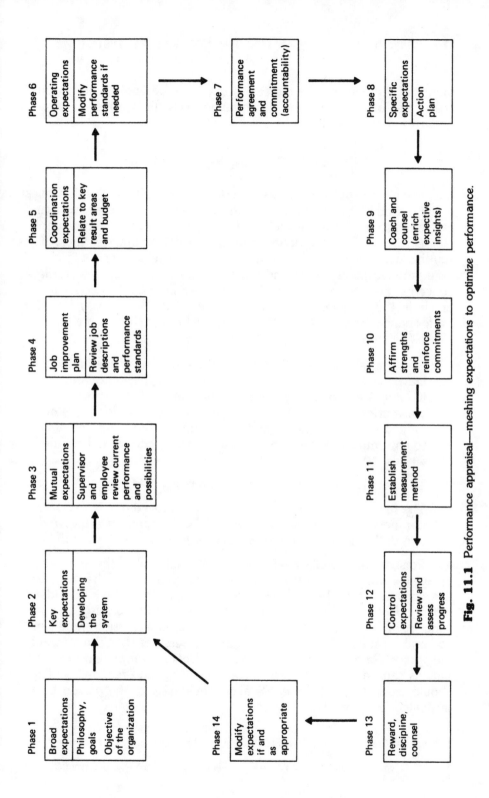

Fig. 11.1 Performance appraisal—meshing expectations to optimize performance.

mance of the person—for the sole purpose of fulfilling the philosophy, goals, and objectives of the organization. This, then, must be clearly understood at the outset.

Phase 2:   Developing the system

It is very important to clearly visualize the pragmatic and ethical realities at the outset. There is, I believe, a vast amount of unnecessary worrying and trepidation about the ethics, prerogative, and other "conscience" factors concerning performance appraisals. This is so unnecessary! And I say this while owing and acknowledging much respect to some of the noted management writers and practitioners who have expressed these concerns. For instance, the highly respected Douglas McGregor in an article in the *Harvard Business Review* entitled "An Uneasy Look at Performance Appraisal" expressed the belief that managers are uncomfortable when they feel they are expected to "play God."

> **. . . the respect we hold for the inherent value of the individual leaves us distressed when we must take responsibility for judging the personal worth of a fellow man. Yet the conventional approach to performance appraisal forces us not only to make judgments and to see them acted upon, but also to communicate them to those we have judged. Small wonder we resist!***

The noted social scientist, Rensis Likert has said

> **The fundamental flaw in current review procedures is that they compel the superior to behave in a threatening, rejecting, and ego-deflating manner with a sizeable proportion of his staff†**

Perspective is badly needed here! Naturally, all of the specters of "playing God," "overdirectivism," "amateur psychiatry," the overreactive converse, "the halo effect," etc. can be realities *if* we do indeed *make judgments.* "You are judgmental" has become a misguided rallying cry of those who really believe that an appraisal session should and can and must *include* judgments. Appraisal sessions should *not* include judgments! Rather, they should utilize *evaluations!* Properly done, evaluations can be constructive, positive, reassuring, and reinforcing. They should speak to the uniqueness and individuality of the person being evaluated and appraised.

---

* Douglas McGregor, 1957 An Uneasy Look at Performance Appraisal, *Harvard Business Review* (May–June): 90.
† Rensis Likert, 1957, Motivational Approach to Management Development, *Harvard Business Review* (July–August): 75.

We must pause here and thoughtfully explore the difference between judging and evaluating.

> Judging — forming an opinion and developing a mindset based on the flaws, weaknesses, or faults of a person, circumstance, or event.

> Evaluating — determining the significance or worth of by careful appraisal and study. Determining or fixing the value of a person, circumstance, or event.

I sincerely hope the reader will perceive implicit in the system shown schematically in Fig. 11.1 a total way of leading, counseling, and developing that is rooted in *evaluation*, the identification and expansion of *strengths* rather than one of *judgment*, the search for and preoccupation with weaknesses. If this approach is properly understood in depth, I feel deeply that the "specters" discussed above need not apply.

Phase 3: Supervisor and employee—review current performance and possibilities

Here are some overall perspectives we can survey as we prepare to understand all fourteen phases of Fig. 11.1:

Questions Employees Can Ask of Themselves Preceding the Interview

1. What are the most important assets I bring to the job I am presently performing?
2. What are the personal development areas in which I most need to improve?
3. What is my timetable for development over the next five years?
4. What have I learned in my work during the past year that will help me most in the future?
5. What can my immediate superior do to help me improve my effectiveness on the job?
6. What would I most like to see changed in the way our department is currently operating?
7. What methods would I recommend?
8. Other than my present assignment, what would I be well qualified to do here?
9. If I were to leave my present assignment, who would I recommend as my successor?

The Purposes of Performance Appraisal

1. To assure an employee a regular, formal opportunity to discuss his or her performance, his or her achievements and difficulties, and his or her goals and expectations.
2. To provide a regular, formal opportunity for a supervisor to discuss his or her view of an employee's performance, present standing, and possibilities.
3. To improve employee performance through recognition, encouragement, constructive criticism, or personal counseling.
4. To establish goals and/or performance standards to be followed until the next evaluation.
5. To offer a periodic formal means of identifying training needs and fostering employee development.
6. To offer a periodic formal means of gathering employee suggestions for improving methods, procedures, performance, practices, and morale.
7. To demonstrate that the employee's contribution matters and that the supervisor is concerned about him or her as an individual.
8. To deepen the employee's job satisfaction and his or her commitment to the organization.
9. To help determine employee potential for advancement.
10. To help provide an objective, equitable basis for making compensation, transfer, and other decisions.
11. To clarify mutual expectations.
12. To provide insight into present and potential strengths.

The Most Common Performance Appraisal Problems

A. Before the interview:
1. Procrastination about scheduling the evaluation.
2. Insufficient or irregular communication with employee. Needed: Shared meaning—shared understanding.
3. Inconsistent follow-up on goals set during previous evaluation.
4. Tendency to take adequate performance for granted and to remember more of the problems in the employee's behavior or performance.
5. Tendency to keep insufficient records on employee performance.
6. Tendency not to plan the interview in enough detail or to allow enough time for it.

7. Tendency not to assess our own contribution to the employee's success or failure in meeting standards.

B. During the interview:

1. Nervousness and difficulty in putting employee at ease or establishing rapport.
2. Failure to structure the interview and inform employee of the rationale of the evaluation process.
3. Rushing or doing too much of the talking.
4. Discussing activities instead of results.
5. Discussing performance in generalities without explaining the "why" of the rating.
6. Avoiding or underemphasizing discussion of genuine performance problems.
7. Getting emotionally involved and losing objectivity and control of the interview.
8. Getting sidetracked or bogged down in details.
9. Overpraising or taking the "sandwich" approach to evaluation.
10. Failure to build on the employee's strengths in developing solutions to performance problems.
11. Failure to involve employee adequately in the planning/goal-setting process.
12. Not listening positively or not pursuing new information or suggestions the employee offers.
13. Using too many negatives.
14. Forgetting that some "facts" may reflect unconscious assumptions or attitudes toward the employee.
15. Comparing employees instead of making individual assessments in terms of potential.
16. Succumbing to the "halo" or "centrist" effect on ratings.
17. Failure to write down all the key points, goals, objectives, and target dates mutually agreed to.
18. Failure to close with a summary that leaves employee with a clear understanding of where he or she stands, what he or she needs to do in the future to meet standards, and how (and when) the supervisor will assist him or her in doing so. In short, failure to establish clearly understood mutual expectations rooted in an understanding of one's strengths.

C. After the interview:

1. Failure to reinforce positive effect of interview with ongoing contact on the job.
2. Difficulty of keeping track of all the follow-up expectations.
3. Tendency to let the average and better employees shift for themselves and concentrate on the employee who is marginal or is creating problems.
4. Tendency to let training and development commitments slide due to the pressures of daily workload.
5. Not enough time to shape employee goals into an effective development plan.

Nuts and Bolts of Performance Appraisal
Tools for Building a Good Appraisal

1. A *job description* gives an item by item list of principal duties, responsibilities, and accountability.
2. *Performance standards* are the conditions which will exist when a job is well done. To establish Performance Standards, determine what is expected, and determine how results can be measured.
3. *Specific objectives and expectations* are mutually established by employer and employee—targets that are realistic, stretching, measurable, and achievable within a given length of time.
4. *An incident file* aids in the recall of good or bad performance, discussed and recorded at the time of happening. It contains clear, specific anecdotes of both positive and negative happenings.
5. *Planning for the appraisal* involves answering the questions: "What results do you want to achieve from the appraisal?" "What contribution is the employee making?" "Is the employee working toward his or her potential?" and "What training does the employee need?"

Rules for Building a Good Appraisal

1. Frequent communication assures that there will be no dramatic *surprises!* Planned *frequent* communication and feedback on the job helps overcome fear *during* the actual performance appraisal.
2. Evaluate your *own* performance before you evaluate the employee's performance. Are *you* responsible for his or her good or bad performance?

3. During a warm-up period:
   a) Take the time to develop rapport and discuss the *advantages* of an appraisal.
   b) Review the *information on hand* to measure the employee's performance.
4. Be candid and be specific. *Candidly* get right to the point in discussing an employee's performance on the job. *Honesty, candor,* and *responsiveness* will result in a big payoff for you and the employee.
5. Build on strengths. This tough-minded approach enables the employee to work toward his or her greatest potential. The employee must use his or her strengths to accomplish a job; he or she *cannot* use weaknesses. Weaknesses are only *absences!*
6. Be a positive listener. Listen with ears, eyes, heart, and entire being. Nonverbal communication often says more than words.
7. Judge performance, not the person. Judge an employee's *performance* and results. Don't judge the person.

Performance Appraisal Standards

A well-written performance standard will meet all or most of the following criteria:

1. *It is specific.* It states specifically the conditions which will exist at the end of the period. There is little reason why all the performance standards of a position, regardless of level, cannot be stated on one page.
2. *It states an end result, not an activity.* There is plenty of time to deal with activities when a plan to meet the standards is developed. Emphasis is now placed on defining results to be accomplished.
3. *It is measurable.* We must know when we reach it, and be able to determine our progress toward it.
4. *It has a targeted attainment date.* While company objectives or goals are usually set for one to ten years in the future, performance standards are usually set for shorter periods. It is the short-range standard that the individual can most easily identify with.
5. *It is practical.* The cost of attainment will be in proper proportion to its contribution.
6. *It is attainable.* Unless people believe the standard to be possible of attainment, their enthusiasm and commitment are weakened.
7. *It should be stretching.* We show our respect for others by looking for and expecting their best.

Performance Standard Format

Criteria: **Standards should be specific, measurable, practical, attainable, have a targeted attainment date, and state an end result.**

Satisfactory performance will be attained when I:
   (VERB)   (SUBJECT)   (END RESULT)   (TARGET)

1. Reduce the number of customer complaint letters from an average of four per month to two per month by October 1, 19____.

2. Reduce turnover in the accounting department from two per quarter to one per quarter by the end of the fiscal year.

3. Qualify two employees in production for supervisory positions by February 14, 19____.

   (To be qualified, an employee must meet the minimum job requirements as outlined in job description and pass company test with a score of 75 percent)

4. Maintain a response time of 30 seconds or less.

   (Response time is defined as the interval between the customer service bell ringing and the salesperson asking customers, "May I help you?")

The Coaching Interview
(Often discussed—seldom done well)

Basic goals and expectations:

1. To help the employee recognize the need to improve performance in a specific area or strengthen a specific job skill or learn a new skill or procedure.

2. To offer information and guidance as needed (including criticism if it is called for).

3. To build on the employee's strengths—to develop them further.

4. To help the employee work out a plan or specific action steps for achieving the desired improvement.

5. To lead the employee to a clear understanding of his or her responsibilities for positive change or correction action and to secure his or her commitment to it.

The Two Basic Types of Coaching Interviews

1. The planned, anticipated, or scheduled interview.

   a) Follow-up interview during the job training period (new job or skill).

b) Feedback interview on job performance prior to formal appraisal.

c) Follow-up interview as agreed to or arranged at most recent performance appraisal or previous follow-up interview (may be based on goals, standards, objectives).

2. The unplanned, unanticipated, or unscheduled interview.

a) Interview dealing with some change in the nature of the job or the employee's usual tasks.

b) Interview dealing with some change in the work environment.

c) Interview dealing with some change in the employee's performance or behavior.

Phase 4. Review Job Description and Performance Standards

Only fairly recently have managers begun to perceive the logic of combining the traditional job description with performance standards. This step forward is overdue! The consolidated documents are designed to reflect *full* performance and thus are certainly indivisible.

Giving Information and Guidance

1. Be honest, sincere, and *real.*

2. Show your respect for the other person by listening more than you talk.

3. Show that you care about the other person's thoughts and feelings.

4. Draw out the other person and be sure you understand his or her point of view and needs before you go any further. Ask, listen, *hear!*

5. Help the other person define the problem for himself or herself by skillful questioning and emphatic listening.

6. Guide the other person to recognize his or her own solution or what he or she needs from you. Positively affirm it.

7. Agree on a mutual course of action to solve the problem or resolve your differences. Be specific.

8. Be supportive, reinforcing, and encouraging. Express confidence in him or her.

9. Emphasize the positive and build on strengths.

10. Follow-up. Keep your commitments to the other person.

11. Expect the best!

The following job descriptions are primarily directive and semidirective.

POSITION DESCRIPTION

Position _____ Class code _____ Incumbent _____ Date _____

Secretary

Department (include sub-
division if appropriate) _____ Reports to first level Title _____
                                 of supervision

Special Health risk

Location   Prepared by _____ Reports to second level
                               of supervision

Home Office

Reviewed by: _____

Incumbent _____ First-level supervisor _____ Second-level supervisor _____

Basic function:
To provide broad secretarial and clerical assistance to officers in the Home Office.

Work performed: Approximate
                                                   percentage of time

Provides secretarial assistance for   50%
officers to include typing and taking
dictation.

Performs wide range of clerical duties such as opening and screening mail, maintaining logs on reports from sales representatives, scheduling appointments and staff meetings, making travel arrangements, answering telephone calls, maintaining diary file, reproducing documents, and completing special projects.

15%

Maintains department attendance records and confidential personnel files. Updates files and business manuals.

10%

Prepares reports and supplies information to personnel, payroll, and other departments.

10%

Maintains reinsurance file for department. Corresponds with reinsurance broker and other company departments in order to update and distribute contracts and addenda.

10%

Communicates with other company staff members and persons outside the company. Requests and provides information relating to company operations.

5%

Job Description for Salesperson

Title: Sales Representative: Health and Beauty Aids
Department: Sales
Supervisor: Manager of Sales
Salary: Grade 3
Date: September, 19___

Purpose: To maintain and increase sales.

Job duties:

1. Maintains quota levels for products in all classes of trade.

2. Sells key accounts on feature promotions, obtaining their support on the retail level to achieve maximum sales during each promotional period.

3. Makes sales calls following prescribed call pattern for each class or trade during each promotional cycle.

4. Conducts a check on retail store sales.

5. Recommends opening of new accounts.

6. Reports to immediate supervisor all competitive activity within assigned territory.

7. Submits prescribed reports to immediate supervisors.

8. Follows up on customer complaints and credit problems.

9. Coordinates the activities of the sales merchandiser.

10. Travels during five-day workweek.

National Bank Job Description

Job title: Manager, customer accounts   Date: _____
Department: Operations division
Supervisor: Vice-president, Operations   Approval: _____

General duties:

1. Responsible for directing, coordinating, and controlling the customer accounts department activities to ensure the effective operation of the department in accordance with established division policies and procedures.

2. Assists in establishing, implementing, and reviewing new methods, procedures, and systems to improve the effectiveness of the bank's operation.

3. Responsible for providing supervision, direction, and control to the assistant manager, senior customer accounts clerk, customer accounts clerk, and mailing clerk.

4. Responsible for the personnel management and administration activities, including but not limited to employment, job assignment, training, performance appraisal, and compensation reviews for personnel reporting to this position, consistent with overall division and bank policy.

5. Responsible for supervising and handling incoming calls from customer and employees and determining appropriate action.

6. Responsible for supervising information retrieval and all required research.

7. Responsible for the preparation of reports required by bank management.

8. Prepares Demand Deposit Accounting (DDA) input for the computer except new accounts and name and address changes.

9. Receives and supervises the distribution of the bank's work from Banks of Iowa Computer Services (BICS).

10. Submits entries to the general ledger for the DDA work.

11. Verifies activity on one-year dormant accounts.

12. Checks posting rejects to detect unauthorized resubmissions.

13. Approves overdrafts or secures approval from other bank officer within established bank policies and procedures.

14. Sends warning letters to customers who abuse their checking accounts; closes those accounts that continue to be abused and reports those that are closed for that reason to Check-It.

15. Performs with the help of BICS account reconciliations of selected accounts.

16. Oversees the activity and maintenance of the copying machine.

17. Assists in business development activities for the development of additional business through new and existing customers and the cross-selling of services.

Job Specification Requirements

Knowledge. This position requires previous work experience in customer accounts or related area with a thorough knowledge of bank procedures, computer language, accounting practices, and customer relations. May require up to two years of training.

Education. This position requires a high school graduate with up to two years training involved with bookkeeping and/ or accounting functions.

Special skills. Requires ability to handle normal office equipment such as microfilmer; adding, folding, and counting machines; copying machine; computer terminal and reader-printer, with basic operational skills.

Personal contacts. This position is responsible for the satisfactory handling of relationships with customers and others having dealings with National Bank. Routine contacts with personnel in other departments.

Resourcefulness. Job duties are standardized and require limited resourcefulness with analytical ability required frequently.

Supervision received. This position is responsible for normal operating decisions with general supervision provided. A supervisor is available when unusual circumstances warrant.

Supervisory responsibility. Responsible for the effective supervision of the employees in the customer accounts section.

Integrity, dependability, and accuracy. Routine access to confidential customer information. Considerable loss of money and customer goodwill could result from inaccuracies or errors in judgment.

JOB TITLE: Administrative assistant
to the President and the
Vice-president of Operations

Date: 5/12/82

DIVISION: Administration

SUPERVISOR: Vice-President of Operations

PURPOSE: To provide responsible assistance to the President and the Vice-president of Operations and aid in the timely and effective execution of their duties and responsibilities.

Duties, responsibilities, and authority	Performance standards	Effective date
Maintain a supplementary engagement calendar for the President and the Vice-president of Operations in order to provide effective support.	Ensure that all necessary information is recorded in a prompt and efficient manner.	
Provide technical, creative, graphic, and written assistance required to develop, design, and complete special projects requested by the President and the Vice-president of Operations.	Ensure excellent quality with prompt turnaround time.	
Communicate information to members of staff in relation to meetings or any other directives as requested by President or Vice-president of Operations.	Prompt and efficient in verbal or memo form.	
Review, process, and file all records and reports required by the Vice-president of Operations.		

Coordinate timely collection of all operating reports and assignments required by the Vice-president of Operations.

Supervisory maintenance of physical facilities.

Remind those with reports and assignments that were not completed on time.

Serve as library resource center coordinator and maintain an effective control to ensure proper working order; order new books as required and approved; catalog all books; circulate memos on new additions to the center; provide constant check on materials to be sure they are being used properly, returned on time, and that proper removals are made of aged magazines, articles, etc.

Ensure that coffee room is kept clean and attractive. Update list of clean-up people.

Keep supply room in clean and orderly condition; assist in ordering supplies.

April—June survey of all magazines, books, periodicals received in office to ensure there is no duplication.

Do initial cleaning by May 22, 1982. Organize in orderly fashion by April, 1982

Drafting policies/procedures under the general direction of the Vice-president of Operations; administer corporate policies/procedures.	Continually renew and update the organizational manual when necessary; replace new or updated policies/procedures in all organization manuals.	
Evaluations, recommendations, and purchase of new office equipment and maintenance of existing equipment.	Maintain contracts and agreements on leased/purchased/rented equipment. Review new equipment of interest with representatives and prepare comprehensive report to Vice-president of Operations for review.	
Coordinate information and maintain personnel records (time sheets, etc.).	Create a file checklist and review and update periodically.	By May 22, 1982
	Create schedule/checklist of performance appraisal times for entire staff.	By May 22, 1982
EEO/AA Plan—Reports—Compliance.	Do necessary follow-through work; keep application flow record up to date.	Learn this plan by May 29.
Interview, selection, and training.	Screen applicants and select best candidates qualified for a particular nonstaff position. Make	Screening for other positions when time permits.

final decision and train receptionist/typist (RT) and mail clerk (MC).

Ensure that RT and MC know/understand his or her job functions/responsibilities. Coordinate the work of both positions.

When necessary review and update RT and MC job descriptions.

Monitor and ensure the timely preparation and completion of assignments and projects that are the primary responsibility of the Vice-president of Operations, obtaining information when recommendations are made for improvement to methods of operation.

Prepare reports and provide analysis and recommendations for solutions of administrative problems.

Coordinate travel arrangements and other arrangements for President's speaking and other engagements.

Development, coordination, security, and maintenance of all filing systems; accountable for all corporate records.

Coordinate or supervise the completion of special projects as assigned by the Vice-president of Operations.

Position Description and Performance Standards
Employee Relations Manager
Management Services Division

OBJECTIVES: To manage the Employee Relations Department by administering management development programs, skills training programs, management trainee programs, on-the-job training programs, wage program, orientation for hourly and salaried employees, exit interviews, position descriptions and standards of performance. To contribute to overall positive attitude of all employees.

Working relationships

Accountable to and reports to: The Director of Management Services

Those accountable to and reporting to the employee relations manager: Not applicable

Receives work from: All employees of company

By:

Approved By:

Date: _____

Duties, responsibilities, and authority

A. Representation of employees

I provide Employee Relations services mainly, but not solely, to M&C, Merchandising, and Planning Division by providing prompt and honest answers, expediting ''Open-door Instances,'' reporting to management problems needing correction, assisting in making consultative management a reality.

Performance standards

Satisfactory performance will have been attained when:

1. I follow guidelines of open-door policy and report and discuss all open doors in which I am involved to the Director of Management Services.

2. I see any employee who wants to see me within 48 hours.

3. I follow up on all questions to ensure that the employee receives an answer.

4. I inform the area supervisor and the Director of Management Services at least every two weeks of all significant information gathered while I am on the grounds.

5. There are no instances in which I have not informed my Director of problems brought to my attention that I cannot resolve.

6. There are no instances in which I have willfully disclosed any information which is asked to be confidential, except when the information concerns an illegal act.

7. I am on the grounds five hours weekly as ''Corporate Conscious.''

8. There are no instances on which I have missed a Corporate or Management Services Divisional Meeting without previously notifying my Director.

9. The Maintenance and Construction, Corporate Planning, and Merchandising Divisions have attained a minimum of 80 percent positive or neutral response on the 1977 Employee Attitude Survey.

Duties, responsibilities, and authority

B. Budget administration

I develop and administer the budget for the Employee Relations Department and authorize expenditures up to $1,500 for any single purchase.

Performance standards

Satisfactory performance will have been attained when:

1. I have submitted a proposed budget to my Director for approval by the agreed-upon date.

2. I do not exceed the approved budget without my Director's approval.

3. I do not enter into any lease agreements or contracts without my Director's approval.

4. I have submitted budget deviation reports to my Director within three (3) working days after receiving the P&L of all variances over $300, or 10 percent—whichever is less—and report the proposed action to bring the account in line.

5. I provide the services to other divisions for which funds were made available.

6. I approve the expense reports for those attending outside training courses and coordinate with Director any questions.

Duties, responsibilities, and authority

C. Team work

I conduct my department in a professional manner, offering my assistance to employees, seeking assistance from other employees, promoting increased productivity within the Management Services division, worked in harmony with my team members, not agreed—upon deadlines and accepted and performed special projects.

Performance Standards

Satisfactory performance will have been attained when:

1. I have met all but four established deadline dates unless an extension has been granted by my Director.

2. I have reported all disagreements I can't resolve to my Director.

3. There are no instances in which I have treated a team member or employee discourteously.

4. There are no instances in which I have failed to assist my team members when asked.

5. I have annually notified my team members of their responsibility in Action Plans for which I am responsible, to include the Divisional Productivity Action Plan. I have reported all instances of nonacceptance to Director of Management Services.

6. I have responded to all assigned projects with a report date within 48 hours unless another date has been assigned or is agreed upon.

7. I have advised my Director of any work I will miss prior to missing the work.

8. I have represented all company employees to the Director of Management Services.

9. I have developed, received approval of, and implemented Strategic Action Plans for my areas of responsibility by the agreed—upon date.

Duties, responsibilities, and authority

D. Hourly wage program

I develop, recommend, communicate, and administer the Hourly Wage Program so that it corresponds with Corporate Guidelines for treating employees fairly.

Performance Standards

Satisfactory performance will have been attained when:

1. I have promoted the fairness and soundness of the Hourly Wage Program.
2. I have conducted the Wage Survey and submitted the Revised Wage Practice by June 1, 19____.
3. I have analyzed all jobs by comparison to other jobs in the company and made grade recommendations to my Director within five days of receiving a recommended grade change.
4. I have answered all questions in regard to the Wage Program within 48 hours.
5. There are no instances in which I have administered the Hourly Wage Program in any manner other than as outlined in the Wage Practice.
6. I have presented one article per quarter in "What's Happening" concerning the Hourly Wage Practice.
7. I have attended one divisional meeting per quarter for the purpose of explaining the Hourly Wage Practice.
8. I have reviewed all status change forms at least annually to ensure the Wage Practice is being followed, specifically:
    a) Employees returning at minimum wage
    b) Employees below midpoint of range
    c) High producers are being paid above the midpoint

    I will notify my Director of my recommendations for any instances not in accordance with the Wage Practice.
9. There are no instances in which I have knowingly revealed information related to any employee's hourly or salaried rate of pay.
10. I have prepared quarterly scattergrams by divisional and corporate areas showing pay of hourly employees on payroll.

11. The response on wage category of annual survey is at least 70 percent positive or neutral.

Duties, responsibilities, and authority

E. Standards of performance

I review and implement the corporate practice on hourly standards of performance per corporate calendar date.

Performance Standards

Satisfactory performance will have been attained when:

1. I have annually reviewed and updated my position description and standards of performance, and they are approved by my Director.

2. I have offered assistance at least annually to the company management team in the development and writing of position descriptions and standards of performance.

3. I have accurate files of 90 percent of hourly position descriptions and standards of performance within 30 days of corporate calendar date.

4. I have annually reviewed all hourly position descriptions and standards of performance to ensure that every effort is made to identify safety responsibilities and prevent serious accidents.

5. I have reviewed at least 30 performance appraisals quarterly to ensure appraisals are made using standards and coordinated deviation with area managers.

6. I have instructed a minimum of one minisession per year in regard to proper utilization of standards of performance as a coaching and counseling tool.

The foregoing examples of position descriptions and performance standards formats are not presented as excellent examples but rather as somewhat typical examples.

Phase 5: Relate to Key Results Areas and Budget

A carefully planned series of questions will help reveal how well the person being appraised understands the relationship of performance standards to the key results areas worked out in phase 4 of Fig. 11.1.

He or she must understand on an intellectual level and, ideally, also on an emotional level how the entire system of expectations, their fulfillment, and rewards work. Oral feedback is a valuable device in this area.

Phase 6: Modify Performance Standards if Needed

In Table 11.2 we see a tool for evaluating performance with regard to standards. It is important to understand a vital management principle here that is too often obscure.

1. Meeting "standard" entitles an employee to something only approximating a cost of living raise. It is needed to *maintain* one's status.
2. Meeting "goal" entitles one to a merit increase of compensation.
3. Meeting "excellence" entitles one to unusual increments in compensation.

Phase 7: Performance Agreement and Commitment (Accountability)

In my book *Tough-Minded Management,* I stated that accountability meant "the clear, warm understanding that you do a job or get out of it." This still holds today. Before this negative portion of the whole balanced concept of accountability is enforced, it places a premium on the excellence of the example and job done by the supervisor. We'll deal with that here, but first, let me clear up the notion that accountability is primarily negative. It is not!

Accountability stipulates provision first of all for rewards for outstanding performance. Only when the desired level of performance clearly cannot be reached does the supervisor take punitive steps.

If the supervisor is a truly tough-minded expective manager, he or she will recognize that organizational authority is to be used as the last expedient rather than the first expedient. Before considering termination or demotion, the supervisor will make sure that he or she has provided the subordinate with

1. The right example
2. The what, where, when, who, how, and why of his or her job expectations
3. The information, training, materials, and resources needed
4. Clear insight into his or her present and potential strengths

Table 11.2 Standards of performance

Job title: _____ Department: _____

Position classification number: _____

Reports to: _____

Prepared by: _____ Date: _____

Definition: Result expected—What the employee is supposed to achieve.

Performance standards—How well the employee is expected to perform.

Performance appraisal—How well the employee is actually performing.

Appraisal key: Excellence—Employee is obviously performing at a level far exceeding the performance standards specified.

Goal—Employee is performing at the level exceeding that expected of a fully qualified individual, exceeding the specified performance standards.

Standard—Employee is performing at the level expected of a fully qualified individual, meeting the specified performance standards.

| | STATUS OF EXPECTATIONS | | |
Meets standard	Meets goal	Meets excellence	Recommended action

5. A clear assessment of his or her possibilities. A weakness is only a too dimly perceived possibility.

6. Some realization of his or her uniqueness and value

7. Above all, warm clarity of expectation

A supervisor who is *truly* tough-minded will have already perceived that poor organizational authority is a poor substitute for *real* authority— the authority of example. Here is a challenge to all managers:

> **I challenge you to manage as though you had no rank—as though you had to depend on the quality of your ideas—expressed through your daily example. Will you do it?**

In this same context, I'd like to quote Ralph Waldo Emerson:

> **What you are thunders so loud I cannot hear what you say.**

For many years I thought that was great. I now believe it was unnecessarily negative and submit the following instead.

> **What you are *can* thunder so loud they'll *want* to hear what you say.**

Phase 8: The Action Plan

We have suggested several kinds of action plans thus far. Here's another one to consider in the context of performance appraisal. See Table 11.3.

Phase 9: Coach and Counsel (Enrich Expective Insights)

Coaching and counseling comprise a crucial part of the whole system for optimizing possibilities and expectations. Before dealing with this very important subject, let's clear up one major deterrent to effective appraisal sessions:

> **Performance appraisal and compensation reviews should be done at separate times.**

because compensation is a means of rewarding *past* performance and performance appraisal is a means of optimizing *future* performance.

We do, indeed, teach that we should "evaluate performance—not the person." But please do not infer that the development of the person should be excluded. *Performance can improve only if the person does!*

Table 11.3 Employee action plan

Key result area: _____

_____

Individual responsible for this activity: _____

_____

_____

Objective: _____

_____

_____

Sequential tasks to accomplish this objective:	By whom	With whom	By when	√

What will be expected by other persons to accomplish this objective?	By whom	With whom	By when	√

Let's move directly into the coaching and counseling session. We provide and conduct such counsel based first on the premise that people (whether they can articulate it or not) are all in some stage of the following three life phases.

Self-discovery
Self-fulfillment
Self-actualization

We premise further that these life phases must receive their basic nourishment from faith, hope, love, and gratitude—the emotional and spiritual foundations of all people.

Please examine Fig. 11.2 very closely and then read it again and again. In Figs. 11.2 and 11.3 are the foundation for expective coaching and counseling. Premising at all times that we ask, listen, and hear, and that we truly care about, enjoy, and see the practical benefits of such face-to-face relationships, we need a deeper understanding of the ten elements in the cyber circle.

- *Examine your strengths.* Until you know your own strengths, you cannot identify, relate to, and optimize the strengths of others. IBM has long known that you must respect yourself or you cannot respect the wants, needs, problems, and possibilities of others.

- *Care.* Without care we have no hope, no zest, no desire to formulate goals and thus no capacity to develop expectations. Caring for others confirms and completes us. We grow in direct proportion to the extent to which we care for others.

- *Listen actively.* Listening with acuity, real curiosity, and wonder adds spice to each moment. It builds insight, friendships, loyalty, and wisdom. It's one mark of a wise and caring person. It permits you to make decisions that are sound and realistic.

- *Find others' strengths.* This can, indeed, become a delightful quest if you are concurrently discovering new strengths in *you*. Because strengths comprise the basis for the only real skills, tools, and, indeed, personhood of others, this diagnostic ability is one important indicator of the manager (on or off the job) who is moving the "craft" of management to the "art" of management.

- *Provide positive reinforcement.* To reaffirm and reinforce behavior and achievement that is right and productive is one of the best ways to help assure that the rightness and productivity will be maintained and, more importantly, continue to increase.

Develop a clear and complete system of expectation in order to identify, evoke, and use the strengths of all resources in the organization—the most important of which is people.

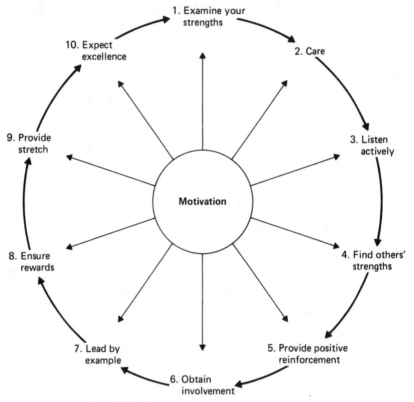

Fig. 11.2 The cybernetic circle of motivation.

- I must learn more of my own strengths and learn to like, yes, and to *love* myself.
- I must care enough about myself and others.
- I must *listen* actively. I must discover wants, needs, and problems.
- I must care enough about others to look for and find their strengths.
- I will provide positive reinforcement and build on strengths.
- I will obtain involvement, input, and jointly agree on commitments.
- I will lead with an example that I will be proud to have others follow.
- I will ensure that rewards are provided in direct proportion to performance and that appropriate steps are taken if commitments are not met.
- I will continue to stretch and discover who and what I really can be.
- I will *expect* the best. *Don't* expect perfection! *Do* expect *excellence!*

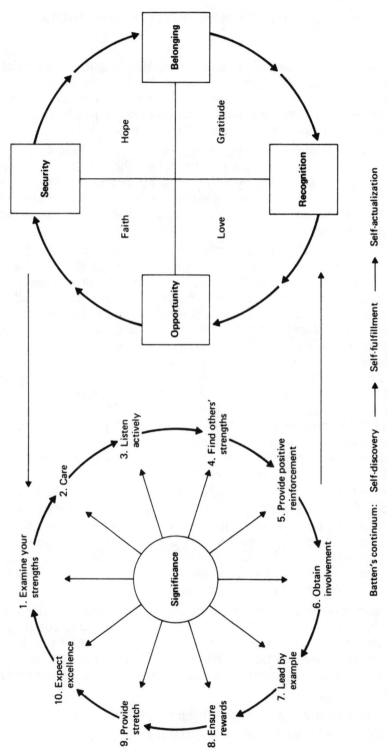

Fig. 11.3 Batten's theory of motivation.

Batten's continuum: Self-discovery → Self-fulfillment → Self-actualization

- *Obtain Involvement.* To obtain participation, input, involvement, is to say, "I really value you and your skills and knowledge; you have something *significant* to contribute." It is essential to unusual cooperative or group achievement. Such agreements, jointly worked out, are much more apt to be carried out with excellence.

- *Lead by example.* Remember my paraphrase of Emerson's comment? "What you are *can* thunder so loud they'll *want* to hear what you say." Leadership by example is by far the most tested and proven form of leadership. Remember the one who simply said, "Follow me." Your own habits and practices as a manager must exemplify *what you expect.*

- *Ensure rewards.* This, of course, is a tangible way to provide positive reinforcement. Rewards mean much more than a modern Pavlovian conditioned response—the carrot and the stick. In addition to the typical quantitative and purely financial rewards, they should be shaped and tailored to unique, qualitative indices of contribution. In the excellent organization of the future, we will see considerably more effort expended to develop imaginative perquisites, even though this development calls for imaginative and facile amendment of typical policies and procedures. For instance, the following qualities should be rewarded: loyalty demonstrated under fire and political stress; stability demonstrated in the midst of organizational confusion and rebellion; hours of work and patience above and beyond the call of duty; resourcefulness and innovation in the face of the fatuous cop-out, "no way . . . ." These qualities and many more must be suitably rewarded.

- *Provide stretch.* It is central to everything in this book that when we look for and expect second best from a subordinate, associate, or family member, we are in effect saying, "I think you are second-rate, I don't *care* enough about you to search for your strengths—your best—and *expect* it." Conversely, there may be no finer way to express respect, love, and tribute to others than to consistently *seek and expect* their best—within reason.

- *Expect excellence.* Here is the stuff of the good life—of uncommon achievement and satisfaction. If we were to list hundreds of great statements of truth and success that the legacy of the centuries has yielded, we would find virtually all of them indivisible with this great expectation. For example, here are some of my own conceptions of truth:

An open mind can grow. A closed mind dies.

Understand life's premises and claim its promises.

The quality inner life leads to the rich and abundant total life.

I will make the lives of others richer by the richness of my own.

I know myself when I know God and you.

To say, "I want to know and use your *best*" is to say "I love you."

To live with a state of wonder may be the nearest thing to a full state of grace.

The word "work" appears 564 times in the *Bible*.

It was not only the "best of times and the worst of times," it was *now* to the joyful.

The total value of you—and of me—is the sum of the values between our ears.

You become what you *think*. You become what you *say*.

Integrity and strength are synonymous.

The shrill and the strident, the hostile and obnoxious are hungry for warmth, love, and affirmation. To respond to these needs may constitute your finest hour.

To strive to be fit mentally, physically, and spiritually is to express a great Amen.

Most people beyond the age of twelve can find at least 200 victories in their lives if they truly seek them.

Creativity can flow only from tension—the muscle tone of the healthy mind and spirit.

Imagine what would happen if the *Sermon on the Mount* were written in everyday language, put in paperback and on *every* paperback display shelf and titled *How to Be a Big Success*.

Two of life's major options are:

> The complex and easy
> or
> The simple and tough.

To be *dissatisfied* is to park beside yesterday's failures.

To be *unsatisfied* is to be hungry for growth, change, and zest.

The go-getter ultimately gets got.

To say, "Everybody's doing it . . . ." means you need more confidence in *your* decisions.

We are defined and profiled by our strengths. Our weaknesses are only what we aren't.

Directive management (living) leaves off where expective management starts.

To allow yourself to exist in a poor state of fitness when there is no medical necessity is to say to your creator: "I reject your gifts. I do not appreciate them."

The biblical injunction, "Judge not that ye be not judged" means to dwell on weaknesses. To *evaluate* another person is to seek to know and evaluate his or her strengths.

Weaknesses *should* be identified in order to determine what additional strengths are needed; or what is needed to further develop existing strengths.

Without profit (richness, abundance) it is difficult, indeed, to propagate good things.

To apologize for an act before doing it is to say: "I'm programming myself to fail."

Enough hate can turn a highly masculine man or a highly feminine woman into an ineffectual neuter.

The more you give of self, the more that self strengthens and grows.

Role orientation is static. Goal orientation is dynamic.

The 1980s can be glorious if enough people *expect* them to be.

Loneliness can be a cause for rejoicing. He who has something in his life to truly *miss* is blessed.

Applied *thought* is the most productive form of labor.

The best "control" is an excellent example.

"Troubleshooters" are usually in trouble with the person in the mirror.

Laughter is more than good medicine. It is life's central elixir.

He who realizes the best from life must consistently expect the best from God, from his neighbor, and from himself.

Vulnerable people grow and change. Invulnerable people ossify and die.

It is impossible to *follow* the person who knows and consistently practices what he is *against* because he isn't *going* anywhere. You can lead only if people follow you or walk with you side by side.

Again, an open mind grows. A closed mind dies.

We have given much attention to phase 9 of Fig. 11.1 simply because it is so important to the effectiveness of all we are trying to accomplish in this book.

Phase 10: Affirm Strengths and Reinforce Commitment

This has already been treated at some length. In the thousands of seminars conducted by Batten, Batten, Hudson & Swab, we place a great premium on specific exercises to understand and use these skills in a specific way. It is all right to counsel the employee on how to better identify, understand, and use his or her strengths. These are his or her tools, that is what he or she is paid for. Performance is accomplished only by people; and performance can be improved only by people who are improving!

Phase 11. Establish Measurement Methods

Is performance appraisal paying off?
Yes _____ No _____

1. What are people doing *to* each other?

_____

2. What are people doing *for* each other?

_____

3. Is work performance improving?_____

How?_____

4. Performance was____ percent.

5. Performance is ____percent.

6. Is there evidence of behavior change?

   a) What? _____

   b) Where?_____

   c) When?_____

   d) With whom? _____

   e) By whom? _____

   f) To whom? _____

g) How? _____
People?_____
Money?_____
Material? _____
Time? _____
Relationships?_____

_____

7. How is the bottom line being affected?
_____

8. Do you and your people mutually understand organizational expectations? _____

9. Do you and your people mutually understand personal expectations?
_____

10. Is there a discernible increase in zest, enthusiasm, morale?_____

11. Do you feel *good* about what's happening?
_____ Why? _____

12. Do you feel *other* than good about what's happening? _____ Why?

13. What is needed for further clarity and excellence of expectations?
_____

14. If changes are needed, think them through and list five.

_____

_____

_____

_____

_____

Phase 12: Review and Assess Progress

Table 11.4 illustrates one kind of aid in carrying out an orderly progress review and assessment.

Phase 13: Reward, Discipline, Counsel

A premium should be placed on the positive reward and actualizing portions of this phase in the context of the meaning previously covered in

Table 11.4 One kind of aid in carrying out an orderly progress review and assessment

Employee accomplishment summary

Employee _____ Period of work _____ to _____

Position _____ Date of assessment _____

Manager _____

Accomplishment compared with expectations	Factors contributing to or detracting from commitment
1.	1.
2.	2.
3.	3.
4.	4.
5.	5.

Coaching appraisal summary

1. How well is your work going? _____

2. What insights, skills, or aids are needed? _____

3. What factors (external or internal) are conditioning performance? _____

4. What changes in commitment, etc., are needed? _____

5. Review or control dates _____

this book. Discipline, or penalty, may be necessary to delineate job or performance accountability, but is minor. We are not using "constructive discipline" because the word discipline is positive in itself. If penalty is considered the minor and latter portion of accountability provisions, it helps this instrument and/or phase to be constructive and productive. We must make no mistake, however, about the sheer fact that demotion, termination, etc. are sometimes absolutely necessary and are a favor for both the organization and the individual.

Phase 14: Modify Expectations If and As Appropriate

As an Olympic gold-medal winner said, "If a thing is not working, do something else!" Accordingly, if expectations are not being met and you have systematically reviewed all of the appropriate steps we have suggested herein, it is possible, indeed likely, that the expectation should be modified. If an examination of the facts suggest this, *do* it! A rigid commitment to expectations that might not be fundamentally right is not tough-minded, it is foolish. Be prepared, of course, to also modify expectations upward when and if this seems appropriate.

Remember:

> **Clear, relevant, stretching expectations are an excellent way to say you care about others.**
> **How much do *you* care?**

Chapter 12

DESIGNING THE SYSTEM

❧✦❧

*IS a system, SHOULD a system, be
a schematically presented assortment
of forms and data built around
a computer?
In stark reality, a system is a
dynamic, ever changing symbiosis
of interacting minds.*

JOE D. BATTEN

Peter Drucker has expressed the feeling that the systems approach, per se, to management has not on the whole worked well. And with this I agree.

The many definitions of system include: "tactics," "scheme," "strategy," and "thoroughgoing." A regularly interacting or interdependent group of items forming a unified whole. A group of interacting bodies under the influence of related forces. The body considered as a functional unit. An organized set of doctrines, ideas, or principles usually intended to explain the arrangement or working of a systematic whole. Harmonious arrangement or pattern. An assemblage of substances that is in or tends to equilibrium. And so on.

I am simply saying, however, that management in general has not worked well *compared with its potential*. For, to seek to differentiate between "system" and "management" is impossible. A system, by its very definition, is virtually synonymous with management.

One of the principal reasons the "systems approach" to management has not delivered its full payload is that it has been thought of in a detached "scientistic" manner. Some thoughts, in this connection, to ponder are:

- A good management organization is a system.
- A poor management organization is also a system, but a *poor* one.

- A key weakness in systems, ergo management, development has been the tendency to view a system simply as an aggregate of materials, of diagrams, flowcharts, "databased modules," equipment and other nonhuman resources.
- A true system, whether management or otherwise, is a gestalt.
- System of values—a complete and functionally compatible combination of essential truths. Values are the subjective interpretation of the immutable laws of the universe which shape and guide human reactions. The orderly expression and transfer of tough-minded values into *practices* is the essential process involved in building a climate of productivity. It is a dynamic interweaving of individual behavior patterns which produces group accomplishment greater than the sum of its parts.*

The system, then, should be conceived as an orderly juxtaposition of resources (people, money, material, time, and space) blended to fulfill expectations of, by, about, and for *people*. This is our central focus. In Fig. 10.1, I have attempted to present an overall expective management system. Let us discuss each of the key elements in turn.

Phase 1: Research

The needs of the total organization must now be sensitively tuned to key events all over the world in terms of external conditioning factors. The six steps that follow must be carefully designed to speak to both these needs and the carefully thought through expectations of the people employed by the organization. The connection now is all too clear between factors that were once thought to be unconnected. For instance, an OPEC action has an immediate effect on our organizational and personal finances and convenience. *Skylab* could conceivably have landed in one's own living room. Organizational research should be considered as a here-and-now kind of thing as well as an ongoing process.

Phase 2: Plan

"Why are we in business?" Or in the case of the nonprofit organization, "Why do we exist?" Surprisingly, most organizations have not taken the necessary steps to scrutinize these questions in a clear-eyed way. Another way of phrasing it is, "What is the *basic utility* we are geared to deliver?" Strategic and tactical planning is for the purpose of addressing the future

* Joe D. Batten, 1965, *Developing a Tough-Minded Climate for Results*, AMACOM.

needs for delivering this basic utility and *making provision and decisions to fulfill these expectations.*

As mentioned previously, the modern expective manager knows he or she can gain additional insights, hunches, clues, and hard data from the entire team if the manager exerts the self-control and discipline needed to truly tap their expectations. The manager knows he or she is accountable for the decisions implicit in the job but wants the best and most realistic future-oriented ideas he or she can get. Above all, the modern executive needs *vision.*

Key questions with profound impact on the future of the organization are set out in response form in Table 12.1.

Phase 3: Organize

Here is where the systematic gestalt begins to come together. Here is a real test for the modern, tough-minded, expective manager.

- Can you truly perceive present and potential strengths in functional design?
- Can you truly perceive present and potential strengths in assessing your team members?
- Can you fit the parts together in a way that is not only a logical synthesis but is also synergistic?
- Does every function make a discernible and somewhat measurable contribution to objectives, goals, and philosophy?
- Will the new organization lend itself to perpetuity and stability?
- Is there sufficient balance of functions and personalities to truly comprise a *team?*
- Lastly, is the key criterion used, one that ensures that the organization lends itself to blended expectations?

Phase 4: Expectations and Execution

In Fig. 12.1 we see some of the real nuts and bolds of expective management. Clear definition of the assignment must be effectively (and concurrently) delegated and communicated in such a way that the subordinate understands the what, where, when, who, how, and why in the specific context of his or her standards of performance.

The subordinate's understanding of the results you expect—his or

Table 12.1 The discipline of planning

Major step	Executive commitment				Criteria	
	Self-control		Commitment to excellence			
	Organization-serving	Self-serving	Very good	Excellent	Expective	Quantifiable
Evaluating						
Involvement						
Commitment						
Philosophy—creed						
Policies						
Key result areas						
Goals						
Objectives						
Strategy						
Tactics						

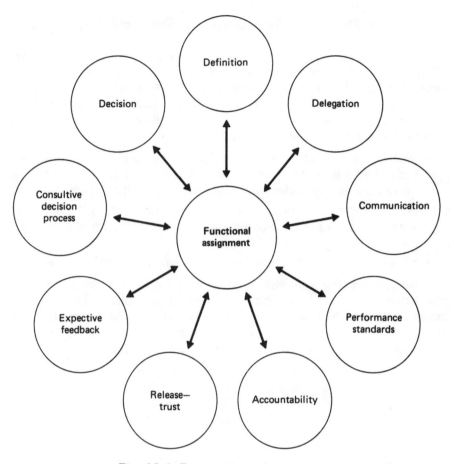

Fig. 12.1 Expectations and execution.

her accountability—should be so thorough that you can exercise full release and trust. Expective feedback, of course, requires that you receive performance information in the form and at the intervals you expect. Consultive or consultative (you decide) decision making is an exercise in democracy, wisdom, and practicality. (See appendix for more on this.) It provides for

involvement + commitment = conviction.

It also allows you to use the best information you can obtain from your team for the purpose of making sound decisions. In sum, it requires that you analyze the alternatives, balance the benefits, and calculate the contingencies.

To effectively carry out the element in Phase 4 requires a sound knowledge of all that has been dealt with previously in this book.

Phase 5:   Coordination (Synergize)

A considerable body of literature has been written about coaching. Some of the mediocre "advice" is overly hortatory and directive. Some is very good. I believe we can confidently expect the emergence of new research, insights, and techniques of expective coaching. It is crucial.

For a team member to experience a positive and developmental coaching experience, it is important that he or she

- Perceives the what, where, when, who, how, and why of his or her present and expected performance. It is particularly important that the team member understands the *why*—the stuff of *real* motivation.
- Feels a strong identification with goals, objectives, and standards. Without such a feeling, nothing approaching optimum coaching will take place.
- Stresses those things about the person which you value (evaluate).

Remember, the total value—present and potential—of a person is the sum of the values he or she perceives and exemplifies. To focus and dwell on the person's or group's weaknesses is not only unproductive, it is counterproductive because it tends to polarize and rigidify the person's behavior and performance into a nonmalleable, nongrowth mold.

You are the sum of your strengths.
You are the sum of your values.
You are the sum of your expectations.
And
they are indivisible!

Phase 6:   Strengths Affirmation

At Batten, Batten, Hudson & Swab, here are some of the things we believe about strengths.

Managementally and managerially, strengths application can be listed in seven ways, and they have been explained and expanded upon in my book *Tough-Minded Management* as follows.

- Strengths identification
- Strengths classification
- Strengths development
- Assignment of strengths
- Synergy and expectations

Strengths measurement
Control of strengths*

If we premise that the deepest need a person has is for *significance,* it follows that our feelings of significance grow in direct relationship to a growing awareness of our strengths as managers and as total people. The converse then is true. When we search for, dwell on, and reiterate the weaknesses of a person, we stultify that person's possibilities, reduce feelings of significance, inhibit growth on and off the job, and seriously hamper performance.

To overemphasize the weaknesses of people is to shackle them with a miserable self-image. To strive diligently and truthfully and very, very consistently to help them know, understand, and *use* their strengths is to *set them free.*

Clear-eyed, objective, and consistent affirmation of strengths becomes one of the great pleasures for the committed expective manager. He or she discovers this adds zest and gusto to the job and the relationships with his or her family.

> *Weaknesses should be identified for the purpose of determining what additional strengths are needed or what is needed to further develop existing strengths*

Phase 7: Control

The term control conjures up visions of massive printouts, computer hardware and software, knitted brows, somber prognoses, and all the paraphernalia of a Management Information System (MIS). And these are indeed important! No real manager questions the value of a carefully and precisely worked out system of budgets. Much of the real value of a budget, however, is the painstaking analysis and study preceding the actual figures. I would like, in addition, to suggest that modern controls should meet two general sets of requirements. They should be

- Economical
- Meaningful
- Appropriate
- Timely
- Simple and operational

Second, it should be understood that the best of all controls is a fused, focused, loyal group of people who know

* Joe D. Batten, 1978, *Tough-Minded Management,* AMACOM.

- What is expected of them
- What they expect

Above all, real control is a system of expectations with calibrated checkpoints that indicate precisely how well the expectations are being met.

Phase 7 flows into Phase 1 and the loop closes—a system of motivation for results fueled and guided by expectations.

Chapter 13

EXPECTIVE RELATIONSHIPS

*Through veils of tears, through mists
of doubt, I can only discover
the reality of you if I
persistently expect your best.*

JOE D. BATTEN

What are relationships designed to accomplish? Why develop "people skills"? Why hone and polish techniques of asking, listening, hearing, exemplifying, clear articulation, etc.? I submit that the central reason will always be to fulfill expectations.

THE REAL LEADER

There is a soul-numbing sameness about much, or most, of what poses for leadership in the world today. The central fault, it seems to me, is one of excessive promises and inadequate or insufficient expectations.

Have the names of any great leaders continued to ring down through history because of "promises" they made? Please think deeply about this. Again:

*Has any person become great
because of promises?*

It does depend, of course, on what we mean by a "promise." Some readers can remember those grim and anxiety-torn days in World War II when the German Wehrmacht was poised on the French coast for a final crushing assault on the "tight little island" of England.

And then, over the radio, transmitted throughout the world, came the gravelly voice of Prime Minister Churchill:

I have nothing to offer but blood, toil, tears and sweat.

This "promise," manifestly, was also an expectation.

Gandhi led a vast underdeveloped country to freedom from under the "British Yoke" and his leadership was notably lacking in the usual symbols and substance of power.

He possessed no economic, political, military, directive, or coercive power. Let's examine his "promise." His *real* power:

You will find yourself by losing yourself in service to your fellow man, your country, and your God.

Was this a promise? I detect nothing herein that implies a chicken in every pot, two cars in every garage, a house with a picket fence in the suburbs, the privilege to die early, glutted by too much to eat, too much to drink, and too many assorted sensual excesses. Instead, he helped pull underfed, underprivileged, generally impoverished people of India out of a preoccupation with themselves and helped them forge an identity, something that *transcended* daily appetites.

Whether anything else was great about the presidency of John Kennedy, only history will show. However, one challenge he gave to the American people (although this quote is widely alleged to have come from Cardinal Cushing and/or others) is powerful and beautiful and will undoubtedly be remembered when all of the New Frontier "promises" are buried in the mists of the past.

Ask not what your country can do for you.

Ask what you can do for your country.

This unleashed a torrent of real commitment and pride. It tapped the finest motives in the human condition. It helped people to feel *good, right, OK* because for one thing it helped them to feel somewhat shrived and cleansed of the cloying, subconscious feelings of greed that nibble corrosively at the vitals of most spiritually flabby Americans.

Most of us are very much aware that we in the United States which has only some 6 percent of the world's population, produce over 50 percent of the world's material wealth.

Note, please, that a comprehensive reading of many, many other great statements of great men and women include the word *ask*. Conversely, practically none of them contain directive, coercive, "telling" statements.

They reflect expectancy, and a commitment to the fulfillment of expectations.

Doubting Thomases among our clients and in our seminars, sometimes say, "These things were OK in the past but now we live in a world of conspicuous consumption and the only way you can motivate people is to promise them more." Do you agree? I disagree completely! In spite of our vast resources and relatively opulent standard of living, there is a hunger in our country that can be satisfied only by a change in attitude, by a change in outlook. There is an unrecognized, growing hunger in our country for stretching goals and expectations as never before. The need for challenge and better standards reposes as a deeply sublimated ache in the hearts of virtually all thinking Americans.

In a newspaper column, Brandt Ayers quoted from a new book *Leadership* by Pulitzer Prize-winning historian James MacGregor Burns as follows:

> **Transforming leadership arises out of a firm sense of the fundamental needs and aspirations of the people, out of great conflict about moral as well as bread-and butter questions, out of a transcending vision or sense of purpose. Perhaps such leadership is impossible in the late 1970s—a time of pervasive self-interest and self-indulgence.**

> **But transforming leaders draw people out of their narrow material concerns; *they often do so less by making promises to followers than by asking for sacrifice from them.* (Emphasis mine.) Many Americans are yearning for leadership today, I believe, but they will not gain it from men who are transfixed by the passage of a proposition 13.**

The columnist, Mr. Ayers, also has this to say about the book by Burns:

> **A presidential adviser recently recommended a book to me that may become a minor classic of American thought—a work that should fascinate and instruct President Carter and anyone who aspires to his office.**

It is such a towering irony, an almost ludicrous conundrum, that there is such a shortage of real leaders who have a desire to lead. I attribute much of this to the specter of directiveness and its insidious ramifications that have been dealt with throughout this book.

We are dealing here with a morass of subtleties, a deep and treacherous Slough of Despond.

People resign from positions and cannot seem to articulate the precise feeling that motivates the resignation. If they are thoughtful, candid, vulnerable people, they often haltingly mention some subliminal kind of fear as the cause—fear of bosses, subordinates, colleagues, family, etc. And this, I submit, is because of a whole ballast of reactions to a directive, self-serving, inner-directed, implosive set of emotional bruises that are products of directiveness.

The resignation from jobs is, of course, only one of myriad happenings that reflect this inward flight that has reached epidemic proportions in our country, indeed in our world.

- We must reach out—not retreat inward.
- We must cherish growth—not the status quo.
- We must understand the universality of the Great Commandment to love God, our neighbors, and ourselves.

Here are forty-seven specific attributes of the tough-minded, expective leader.

EXPECTIVE MANAGEMENT VALUES AND PRINCIPLES FOR LEADERS

Applied Thought Leaders believe this is the most practical form of labor.

Self-Discipline They practice self-discipline in terms of legal and ethical rules of conduct. They recognize that a vigorous, outgoing, and sometimes ebullient way of life can be possible and lasting only as a product of such discipline.

Physical Fitness Leaders recognize that developing and maintaining maximum physical fitness is an important requisite of mental health and acuity; that such fitness is not self-indulgence but part of executives' obligation to their business, their employees, and their family. They become a bit of an authority on it and encourage their subordinates to do likewise. The development of the whole person is just lip service, they believe, without follow-through in terms of physical well-being. They expect to feel well.

Enjoy Life They enjoy life—and people know it! Dour, scowling, formidable executives gain little by their behavior except ulcers for their staff and themselves. They are impatient with the type of people that feel a harried expression and an ulcer are signs of success. They know these people must grow up. They think laughter is great. They expect to laugh and to hear laughter.

Broad Perspective Their interests and activities may range widely or may center in certain worthwhile areas. At their best, truly broad gauge executives read widely and have their own private development program. They feel that a broad and eclectic fund of knowledge makes not only for a better generalist but also for a better specialist. They see the broad picture. They look beyond their own specialities or departments to think in terms of the customer, who is the *ultimate* reason for their job.

Faith in Self and Others They believe that we are the sum of our strengths and that the only *real* things to search for, relate to, and believe in are the strengths of one's self, one's God, and others. They *assume* there is positive evidence of things that are still unseen.

Positive Thinker They take the stand that negativism is never justified. They know that there are pluses and minuses in many situations but that the minuses can become pluses. Minuses are really only the absence of pluses.

Desire to Learn They cultivate a curiosity for new dimensions of knowledge and resist efforts to predicate plans on past and present knowledge only. They do not confuse wit or intelligence with wisdom and strive for greater wisdom.

Enjoy Work They know life without work is a shortcut to deterioration, that work—hard positive work—is one of life's great renewing agents.

Generate Enthusiasm They do not look to others to charge their battery but takes the necessary action to internalize perpetuating values, inspiration, and intellectual enrichment. They retain their sense of wonder. They let their innate love of life, their acquired exuberance, show. They believe it is crucial to "get a lot done and have a lot of fun" and know the two are indivisible.

Not Deterred by Small People They are not deterred by small people. They know what they want and expect and what the organization needs. They secure maximum participation from their key people, and move ahead resolutely toward the actual practice of management by integrity.

Build on Strengths They build on strengths. While they recognize that they as well as all people have weaknesses, their primary concerns are the strengths of people because it will be strengths—not weaknesses—that will make their organizations thrive.

High Expectations They *stretch* themselves and their people. While they never expect more from a person than that person is capable of performing, they often expect more than that person believes he or she can accomplish. This is their key for developing the confidence and ability in individuals and helping them to obtain a maximum feeling of accomplishment.

Goal-Oriented Since a straight line is the shortest distance between two points, they know we must have some future point clearly in mind, or we dissipate and vitiate our efforts.

Significance They know people can truly live and grow only if they feel *real*, if they can experience faith, hope, love, and gratitude.

Openness "Let other people in and let you *out.*" Leaders believe that the absence of defensiveness is an indication of strength and management maturity.

Warmth They reach out to people and do not simply sit back and wait. They demonstrate caring and concern. Their voice and manner project relaxation and positive concern.

Consistent Leaders meet commitments, keep their word, and can be *relied* upon. They *expect* this from others.

Team Synergy This occurs when the effort of two or more people adds up to a whole that is greater than the sum of the parts.

Unity A fused and focused oneness of purpose, effort, and direction.

Caring Leaders literally want others to grow, benefit, and become enriched.

Positive Listening Leaders are *positive* listeners. They keep an open and flexible mind. Because they encourage creativity within their organizations, they listen positively to ideas that are presented trying to discover ways the ideas will work.

Enrich Lives of Others Leaders are proud of their lives and seek to enrich the lives of others by the richness of their own.

Live Integrity They live integrity instead of relying on preachments. They know that management by integrity is realistic and workable; that, in reality, there is no fit substitute for it.

Emphasize Results, Not Activity Tough-minded managers concentrate on results rather than activity. They measure the performance of their subordinates in terms of results and their contribution to company objectives. They believe that people are on the payroll for one reason only—to make a significant contribution to company objectives.

Practice Candor They practice candor wisely and reflect a true warmth of feeling toward their associates. They have the courage to say what ought to be said. They realize the time for permissiveness and apologistic behavior by managers is long past (if it was ever appropriate).

Manage by Example They know that the actions of a responsible executive are contagious and that there is virtually no limit to potential accomplishment if a sufficient number of people *live* the precepts of tough-mindedness.

Have Defined Their Philosophies They take steps to ensure that their organizations' philosophy, objectives, and standards are researched, developed, and clearly communicated.

Define Results Expected They know that people are more efficient and happy when they understand clearly what results are expected of them.

Develop People They believe and live the concept that the development of people, as a whole and in depth, pays real dividends to both the business and the individual. They make certain that the statement, "Management is the development of people, not the direction of things," moves briskly beyond the lip-service stage and becomes completely understood and operational.

Provide Purpose and Direction They know that all personnel will contribute and receive more if they are helped to develop a clear feeling of purpose, direction, dignity, and expectations. Leaders provide *direction,* not *directions.* They explain very thoroughly *what* they want, but leave the *how* up to their subordinates.

Age of the Mind They define management as, "An ever-changing, ever-dynamic system of interacting minds."

Manage Change They know that changes in business and the world in general are inevitable, but they don't resist them. They anticipate the unfolding of the future, plan for it, and set trends. They require and encourage a climate conducive to innovation and creativity in all facets of the business.

Relate Compensation to Performance They believe that providing rewards for seniority, long hours, education, and old school ties denies the dignity and worth of the individual. They care too much for people not to *expect their best* and pay them *for positive performance.*

Unsatisfaction They are hungry for improvement, growth, and "a better way."

Flexible They abhor rigidity in all policies, procedures, and attitudes. They know hardness and weakness are usually synonymous.

Go-Giver They believe that the more one puts into—or *gives*—to life and one's work, the more one receives. Also, life becomes a pleasure.

Involvement They seek the *involvement* of their people in developing goals and plans, not only because they want to utilize all the talents within their organization but also because they know that people will identify better, become enthusiastic and *committed* about meeting objectives if they have a part in *determining them.*

Climate for Mistakes They have the courage to let people make mistakes. By recognizing this need they also become better delegators. They believe in the right to succeed and the freedom to fail!

Provide Psychic Wage They provide for a psychic as well as a real wage for their people because they recognize the psychological needs of people, as well as their physical needs.

Make the Complex Simple They constantly strive to make the complex simple. They know settling for a complex solution is settling for second best.

Guard Time They guard their time carefully and allot it to key areas where it will produce the greatest impact. Because there are so many tasks to be done, they concentrate their time and energy on doing one thing at a time and doing first things first. They set priorities and stick to them even if that means secondary things do not get done at all.

Understand People They continually strive to attain a better understanding of people and their differences—to determine what it takes to impel each person to produce and create. They recognize that many people need to be stretched, helped, encouraged, and yes, sometimes pressured to reach out and grasp the opportunities that lie all about them.

Vulnerable They clearly perceive the degenerative effect of living behind one's defenses. They know we must open ourselves to life, events, and people in order to grow and improve.

Need for Respect They believe it is possible to be both respected and liked, but realize that respect is primary. They know that they cannot be all things to all people and expect to have to deal with unpleasant situations.

They *expect* rather than *insist*. Expectations stretch, open, strengthen, motivate, and "turn on." They should be kind, caring, and *firm*. Insistence pushes, compresses, represses, and depresses. It is often cold, impersonal, and expedient.

They are deeply interested in *the fundamental needs and aspirations of people,* not because of some abstract eleemosynary sense of "nobility," but because they really care, enjoy, and are renewed by such concern. Thus their lives constantly expand, deepen, and enrich.

Grace Grace is a special warmth felt and expressed toward all other human beings; an absence of pettiness and self-concern. It is a living manifestation of the belief that one should devote all one's major energies to doing something *for* others and not *to* others.

Tough-Minded They are flexible, pliant, lasting, durable, high-quality, difficult to break; expanding, strengthening with experience. The tough-minded personality has an infinite capacity for growth and change.

HOW PRACTICAL IS ALL THIS?

I don't really know of anything that endures and continues to provide utility, pleasure, service, profit, and other good things that is a product of all-out directiveness.

For instance, a building is a permanent structure of metal, glass, mortar, and mechanisms. Could this have been a creation of a whole series of directives? I think not! If it is, indeed, a structure of strength and integrity, of design and function, it required some very clear overall expectations and many expective components or it would be second-rate displaying no pride of craftsmanship, no immersion in purpose.

You have probably heard of the story of the three workers on a construction site who were asked, "What are you doing?" One said, "I am laying bricks." The second said, "I am building a wall." The third said, "I am building a beautiful cathedral." Which one do you think was doing what he had been directed to do? Which one do you think was doing what he had been expected to do? Which one's *practices*, accordingly, were the most *practical*? Which way do you want to live, work and *lead*?

It's up to you!

EXPECTIVE MENTAL HYGIENE

Leaders who will and can truly lead must feel right about relationships. I include here, sweepingly, their relationships with—their feelings about—themselves, their fellow creatures, and their God. While this is in no sense intended to be a theological treatise, I find I cannot in all conscience deal with what I believe to be the greatest contributor to mental health and hygiene of all human values without dealing with

Forgiveness.

Please note that I am not contending that one has to be "religious" to be able to forgive. It might be insightful, however, to note that if one goes to the heart of the Gospels of the New Testament, one finds the *Sermon on the Mount* as chronicled by Matthew. At the heart of this great compendium are

Missions	Objectives
Philosophy	Standards of performance
Goals	and
Key result areas	Accountability

All of these are suffused with forgiveness.

One finds that gratitude and forgiveness comprise the essence of love, tough-minded, agape love. We have previously dealt with gratitude. Here are some thoughts for leaders who know they must attain a high level of emotional, mental, and spiritual integration and sense of well being:

- One cannot truly forgive and forget. One only sublimates the part one wants to forget. It's still there!

- One must *remember* before one can forgive. One must confront the fact—the reality of the thing—needing forgiveness.

- A personal philosophy of forgetting consigns one to a life of adequacy at best (although it is through misinformation, the norm) to sublimation of resentments, the "martyr complex," and other unhealthy conditions.

- A personal philosophy of forgiving if diligently practiced, ultimately allows one to feel a healthy measure of forgiveness *toward* and *from* one's God, one's fellow person, and oneself.

I cannot overemphasize the cleansing, freeing-up, growth-inducing value of learning to truly forgive. There are far too many to whom revenge is sweat and vindictiveness is a crutch. This can, and has, countless times caused all forms of bitterness, conflict, personality disintegration, and just plain unhappiness.

To truly lead, will you respond to this challenge?

> **Will you build a life-style of being**
> **for giving and shun the expedience of**
> **seeking only to take and get?**
> *You decide!*

Chapter 14

BUILDING THE EXPECTIVE TEAM

⟨⟨◆⟩⟩

*The mortar of greatness in
teambuilding is individual
commitment to shared goals
which transcend individual
wishes.*

JOE D. BATTEN

The Alpha and the Omega of management accomplishment is the management team. Much has been written and said in recent years about "team building" and many esoteric devices have been proffered. As a term and concept, it is virtually in the same hazardous position as "organization development." Reduced to "OD," organization development has often become an amalgam of experimental academic interplay having little to do with *developing the organization to fulfill expectations.*

So, away with the gobbledygook! Let's discuss team building as a set of *managerial* devices. This treatment may sound almost identical with organization development because the two should, in general, be considered indivisible.

THE TEAM CONCEPT

The excellent team has tempo, defined as

The speed with which an organization identifies problems and opportunities and makes and implements decisions.

I believe that an excellent team possesses these qualities and more. They include

- An attitude that is flexible, durable, open, growing, questing, vulnerable, and expective.

- Clear, properly developed goals and objectives.
- Building on strengths—the only tools an organization or individual possesses.
- A readiness to take on new and different challenges, problems, and opportunities.
- Caring—the capacity and desire to *feel* for people, events, and circumstances.
- Accountability—feeling truly answerable for your actions as a leader and team member.
- Significance—uniqueness; realness.
- Synergism—the capacity to compound resources for positive results.
- Candor or applied integrity.
- Communication: shared meaning—shared understanding.

Some key components of human understanding and interaction include

- Self-confidence and esteem. Without these feelings we cannot fully trust and esteem members of the team.
- Integrity and strength are identical. The strength of a relationship is its integrity and vice versa. This is a fascinating idea to think about because the two words are often used in quite a different context.
- A vital and significant concept of self. The Golden Age of Greece was a direct product of a concept of self that was the wellspring and nourishment of the great intellectual and architectural achievements of that era. The Greeks believed that if one hurts another, one hurts oneself. They believed, further, that if one sought truth and beauty in another, *one found these same qualities in oneself.* The self was made whole and complete only in caring and synergistic relationships with others.

When that beautiful—and eminently practical—concept of self shrank back into a narcissistic preoccupation with one's own body, mind, and spirit, the tough-minded substance that constituted the Golden Age of Greece crumbled.

The basic framework of expective team building (ETB), or you may wish to consider it as expective organizational development (EOD), is shown in Fig. 14.1. You will readily perceive the similarity of Fig. 14.1 to other schematics in this book; however, this figure is devised with a team-building, organizational development emphasis.

Next, please figuratively superimpose over Fig. 14.1 the elements shown in Fig. 14.2, the Cybernetic Circle of Motivation.

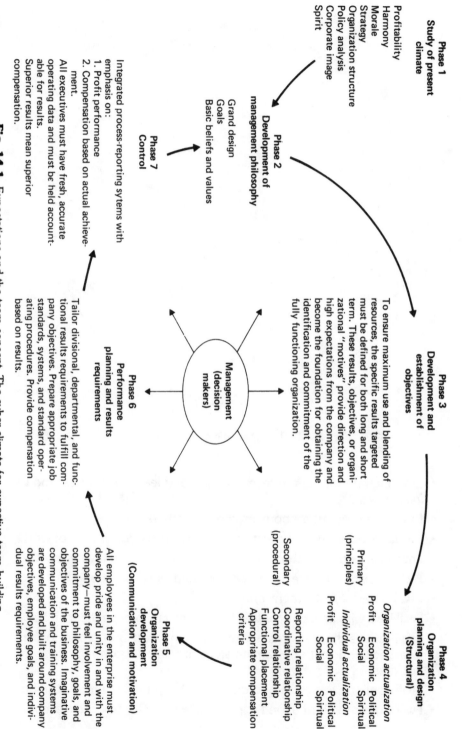

Phase 1
Study of present climate

Profitability
Harmony
Morale
Strategy
Organization structure
Policy analysis
Corporate image
Spirit

Phase 2
Development of management philosophy

Grand design
Goals
Basic beliefs and values

Phase 7
Control

Integrated process-reporting systems with emphasis on:
1. Profit performance
2. Compensation based on actual achievement.
All executives must have fresh, accurate operating data and must be held accountable for results.
Superior results mean superior compensation.

Phase 3
Development and establishment of objectives

To ensure maximum use and blending of resources, the specific results targeted must be defined for both long and short term. These results, objectives, or organizational "motives" provide direction and high expectations from the company and become the foundation for obtaining the identification and commitment of the fully functioning organization.

Management (decision makers)

Primary (principles)

Organization actualization

Profit   Economic   Political
Social   Spiritual

Individual actualization

Profit   Economic   Political
Social   Spiritual

Secondary (procedural)

Reporting relationship
Coordinative relationship
Control relationship
Functional placement
Appropriate compensation criteria

Phase 4
Organization planning and design (Structural)

Phase 6
Performance planning and results requirements

Tailor divisional, departmental, and functional results requirements to fulfill company objectives. Prepare appropriate job standards, systems, and standard operating procedures. Provide compensation based on results.

Phase 5
Organization development (Communication and motivation)

All employees in the enterprise must develop pride and unity in and with the company—must feel involvement and commitment to philosophy, goals, and objectives of the business. Imaginative communication and training systems are developed and built around company objectives, employee goals, and individual results requirements.

Fig. 14.1 Expectations and the team concept. The cyber-climate for expective team building.

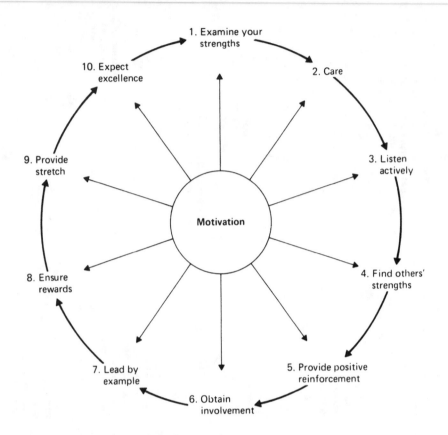

Fig. 14.2 The cybernetic circle of motivation.

- I must learn more of my own strengths and learn to like, yes, and to *love* myself.
- I must care enough about myself and others.
- I must *listen* actively. I must discover wants, needs, and problems.
- I must care enough about others to look for and find their strengths.
- I will provide positive reinforcement and build on strengths.
- I will obtain involvement and input.
- I will lead with an example that I will be proud to have others follow.
- I will ensure that rewards are provided in direct proportion to performance and that appropriate steps are taken if commitments are not met.
- I will continue to stretch and discover who and what I really can be.
- I will *expect* the best. *Don't* expect perfection! *Do* expect *excellence!*

Please study and restudy the components of each. Challenge them, try to improve them.

Expect to do so!

BUILDING TEAM VITALITY

Many years ago when writing the first edition of *Tough-Minded Management*, I stated on the very first page:

> **. . . and the first ingredient, it seems to me, is vitality. Innovation, creativity, tough-mindedness, and, in the final analysis, end results are not possible without it.**

I cannot say it better today!

Some problems or deficiencies currently having adverse effects on building teams are

- The failure to realize that an objective, a motive, and an expective are virtually the same. We feel that interpretations of the word "objective" have done much to shortchange the motivational and fulfillment possibilities inherent in it.
- Too many team members do not understand the what, where, when, who, have, and above all, the why of their jobs and their organization.
- Lethargy, politicking, apathy, inefficiency, work of poor quality, and just plain lack of caring because management has not provided and exemplified sufficient purpose and direction.
- Leaders who live, talk, and work in terms of what they are against instead of what they are *for*.

To instill vitality, we need

- A mutual feeling of caring about each other.
- To be vulnerable, open, and receptive to the wants, needs, and problems of others.
- To reduce the amount of "telling," that is, abrasiveness, directiveness, pushing, and crowding. In contrast, take the word "tell" and turn it around so that it becomes "let." I do not mean slipshod permissiveness. I mean, rather, to let team members feel part of a strong expectation-oriented approach.
- An example that ". . . thunders so loud I *want* to hear what you say."

- A vital style and tone that comes from the Chief Executive Officer through the Chief Operating Officer and permeates the entire team. At Batten, Batten, Hudson & Swab, we have a light-hearted slogan which says:

    > Try to stay within sight of my heels
    > and we'll get a lot done and have a
    > lot of fun! And you can't do much
    > of one without the other!

- One of the best possible ways to express dedication to your team is clear and stretching expectations. I believe that when you care enough about a person to find out his or her best qualities, encourage these qualities, and expect commitment and conviction, you are showing dedication, respect, and yes, even affection, that is *real*.

- All of the other elements are described in Fig. 14.2, the Cybernetic Circle of Motivation.

BUILDING A CLIMATE OF RECEPTIVITY

It has been pontifically propounded from coast to coast, in boardrooms, the hot-stove league, and the rubber-chicken circuit, that "people don't want to change" or that "people don't like to change" or that "people will always *resist* change." Nonsense! People act that way or *seem* to act that way because all too many have been conditioned to feel "that's just the way it is." They display a sheeplike tendency to buy the status quo.

I believe deeply that, in reality, all relatively normal people *want, need, require,* and *expect* change. Virtually all, and possibly all changes initiated by any such relatively normal people are for the precise reason of desiring or seeking change. Even if the action appears to be a decisive step to avoid something in the offing, that person's action is designed to change whatever is happening to her or him.

The expective manager premises that organizational and behavioral changes will be well received if the proper preparation has taken place. Such preparation implies:

- That there is more than adequate *why* supplied.
- That expectations are clear and logical enough.
- That sufficient participation, involvement, and input occurred.
- That team members do not feel simply "What am I going to get out of it?" but rather "What can I put into it so that we'll all benefit?"
- That team innovations are exemplified and come down from the top.

- That consistent and enlightened feedback is received concerning what progress is being made.
- That the objectives were broadly conceived, thoughtfully planned, executed, measured, and evaluated.
- That team members feel a *sense of mission*—a feeling of being part of something bigger than themselves. For a time it is sufficient to simply advise them of growing or increasing profit, but that will not sustain and increase motivational momentum *unless* they can relate to the other three dimensions of profit as shown in phase 4 of Fig. 6.1.
- That the team members feel *significant.*

VALUES—ORGANIZATIONAL AND INDIVIDUAL

In a very real sense this entire book is intended as a treatment of values. The value of an organization is the *sum* of the values thought, taught, and wrought therein.

Everything depends on the value system. The value of the team is directly dependent on the values that it stands for, its components, and the extent to which it is understood. Introduce second-rate values into a team—particularly through the leader—and you will share a second-rate team. Introduce stretching, dynamic, first-rate values and—while it may not happen overnight—you will ultimately have a first-rate team.

TECHNIQUES OF TEAM BUILDING

Some key factors, techniques, and considerations in effective team building include

- Sound and relevant research regarding wants, needs, and problems.
- Take time to truly define what you want or expect to accomplish.
- Stress the right example.
- Allow for differences in the personalities, ambitions, and attitudinal sets of team members.
- Develop consensus and unanimity.
- Steady feedback to provide progress data, recognition, feelings of belonging, and significance.
- Stress the importance of each manager acquiring greater skill in asking legitimate, caring questions.

- Be sure to teach how infinitely more powerful a question is than a declarative statement in terms of practical persuasiveness.
- Seek to insure the mutuality of motives and expectations of all members of the team.

CHALLENGES AND BENEFITS

Some challenges

- Personality conflicts
- "Abominable no-man"
- Diffusion of effort
- Defensiveness and rigidity

Some benefits

- Greater productivity
- Higher morale
- Upbeat habits
- Candor and openness
- Vulnerability to new ideas, experiences, growth, and change
- Better cooperation and coordination
- Synergy
- Greater camaraderie and esprit de corps
- A greater feeling of caring, sharing, and more profit
- Greater individual and organizational actualization

Do you want a *team* or a diffused *group?*
Do you want system and order or management by crises?
Do you want to *manage* or merely *cope?*
Do you want your expectations to be met?
You decide!

The summit of human experience is to impart and share a vision of what can be—a magnificent expectation.

Chapter 15

THE PROFESSIONAL EXERCISE OF POWER

*Great power should never
be vested in those who
compulsively seek it.*

JOE D. BATTEN

In the final analysis, this is a book about leadership—about leading. If we seek to *drive* our lives, we begin to close off corridors in the mind, in the spirit, and in the work place. In the sense that I alluded to in the great poem "The Hound of Heaven," we flee from our possibilities, our potential, and our dreams. All too often we live life at the level of craft at best and never even get a whiff of the *art* of living.

THE TRUE NATURE OF POWER

Conversely, regardless of religious beliefs or, perhaps, their complete absence, if we perceive the unlimited vistas which exist for us when we understand the great expectives which we have all been given:

Ask and it will be given you
Seek and you will find $\Big\rangle$ = **ASK.**
Knock and it will open unto you

We begin to perceive, however dimly, that life is not for pushing, crowding, insisting, driving, coercing, and directing.

Rather, we are presented with the magnificent expective to *lead*—to pull, stretch, reach, grow, change, confront and, above all, to *expect the best*. This is the stuff of true leadership. All of the truly great leaders of history were masters of the art of clarifying and communicating expectations. The Great Expecter stepped into human history almost two thousand years ago. The validity of His message has been wrought on the anvil of human trial and error. No one need drown in the midst of freedoms in the expective world of tomorrow.

A leader, of course, has power. A true leader, not a forcer or driver, usually has more power than he or she even fully perceives. The professional exercise of this power is often an awesome responsibility.

John W. Gardner, author of such superb books as *Excellence* and *Self-renewal* has some challenging things to say about power and its use.

> Very few of our most prominent people take a really large view of the leadership assignment. Most of them are simply tending the machinery of that part of society to which they belong. The machinery may be a great corporation or a great government agency or a great law practice or a great university. They may tend it very well indeed, but they are not pursuing *a vision of what the total society needs. They have not developed a strategy* (emphasis mine) as to how it can be achieved, and they are not moving to accomplish it.

> Scientific and professional people are accustomed to the kinds of problems that can be solved by expert technical advice or action. It is easy for them to imagine that any social enterprise could be managed the same way. They envisage a world that does not need leaders, only experts. The notion is based, of course, on a false conception of the leader's function. *The supplying of technically correct solutions is the least of his responsibilities.* (Emphasis mine.)

> People who have never exercised power have all kinds of curious ideas about it. The popular notion of leadership is a fantasy of capricious power. The top man presses a button and something remarkable happens. He gives an order as the whim strikes him and the order is obeyed.

> The capricious use of power is relatively rare except in some large dictatorships and small family firms. Most leaders are hedged around by constraints—tradition, constitutional limitations, the realities of the external situation, rights and privileges of followers, the requirements of teamwork and, most of all, the inexorable demands of large-scale organization that does not operate on capriciousness. We are immunizing a high proportion of our most gifted young people against any tendencies to leadership. The process is initiated by the society itself. The conditions of life in a modern, complex society are not conducive to the emergence of leaders. The young person today is acutely aware of the fact that he is an anonymous

member of a mass society, an individual lost among millions of
others. The processes by which leadership is exercised are not
exceedingly intricate. Very little in his experience encourages
him to think he might some day exercise a role of leadership.
This unfocused discouragement is of little consequence
compared with the expert dissuasion the young person will
encounter if he is sufficiently bright to attend a college or
university. In some institutions today the best students are
carefully schooled to avoid leadership responsibilities.*

What a damning indictment of our society! So much of this passive
malaise toward leadership and power is so unnecessary. The eagerness
to learn about leadership is there. I may appear to be disagreeing with Dr.
Gardner (although I agree with most of what he says) when I share with
you that during the current year approximately 3,000 seminars will be
held in North America by Batten, Batten, Hudson & Swab and enroll-
ment will average from twenty to forty people in every seminar.

Why are people responding in such impressive numbers? We believe it boils down to roughly three things.

- They want to gain an increment of *hope* in their jobs and their lives
  as a whole.
- They want to know more about how to discover the powers within
  them and use them wisely.
- They want to fulfill newly surfaced and perceived expectations. They
  want to count for something!

Again, let's tune in on what Dr. Gardner says with such cogency and
excellence.

We don't need leaders to tell us what to do. That's not the
American style of leadership in any case. We do need men and
women in every community in the land who will accept a
special responsibility to advance the public interest, root out
corruption, combat injustice, and care about the continued
vitality of this land. We need such people to help us clarify and
define the choices before us.

We need them to symbolize and voice and confirm the most
deeply rooted values of our society. We need them to tell us of
our faithfulness or infidelity to those values.

And we need them to rekindle hope. So many of us are defeated
people—whatever our level of affluence or status—defeated

* From pp. 126–128, 134 in *No Easy Victories* by John W. Gardner. Copyright © 1968 by John W.
Gardner. Reprinted by permission of Harper & Row, Publishers, Inc.

sometimes by life's blows, more often by our own laziness or cynicism or self-indulgence. The first and last task of a leader is to keep hope alive—the hope that we can finally find our way through to a better world—despite the day's action, despite our own inertness and shallowness and wavering resolve.

The professional use of power requires:

Purpose and direction	Dignity
Vulnerability to positive insights	Integrity
	Judgment or wisdom
Growth and wonder	Courage
Caring	Faith
Excellence of example	Love
Excellent work habits	Hope
	Vision

The possibilities implicit on planet earth are enormous, much greater than any of us can currently perceive. The possibilities in the minds and spirits of people are truly the new frontier. Let us mine those riches. Let us dare to expect the best!

Will you?

APPENDIXES

APPENDIX

WHAT IS THE LATEST THINKING ON THE ART OF DECISION MAKING?

Question: What is the latest thinking on the art of decision making? Of what importance is a manager's ability to make decisions?

Joe: When all is said and done, this is really all that the manager gets paid for. I'd like to put that in perspective or in context. I believe that the only usable, effective resource that individuals take to work each day to achieve their responsibility to make objectives happen, is themselves. The applied use of their minds is another way to say "what they are paid for." But the way in which they use their minds to achieve objectives, through making decisions, is what it's all about. An interesting little departure here: At this point in time many people still have a tendency to say, "Well, what does a system of values have to do with solid, practical, realistic management?" I'd like to put it this way: A good many times, somebody has said to me, "You know, Joe, I think that is a value judgment." And I say, "Can you give me an example of any kind of judgment that is *not* a value judgment?" And of course no one can because *every* judgment that we make is the product of the values we hold as individuals. A judgment is also a decision. How practical can you get when you recognize that the one thing that a manager is really paid for is to make decisions and to make objectives happen because of those decisions. Decisions are only as effective as the quality of the manager's personal values.

Question: Is the ability to make snap decisions—spur-of-the-moment decisions—important for the good manager?

Joe: I know some executives who make a lot of decisions very rapidly. Their colleagues and subordinates are pretty impressed by this. What they usually fail to note is that the executives have spent years doing their homework. They have utilized broad and specific patterns of reading, intellectual curiosity and growth, and research, both on and off the job. They are constantly taking in information. You might say they are kind of a walking sponge. They are interested in a lot of things. Out of this broad arsenal of general information, they are able, after doing homework in terms of the specific objectives of their jobs and their companies, to make decisions that are crisp, firm, and unfaltering, but they are seldom snap decisions.

Question: Like the decision of a computer, it comes in a millisecond, but it has had an enormous resource of material to draw from.

Joe: Absolutely. And today with the skilled, realistic, and practical use of the computer, we find many executives who are clued in each day very thoroughly on operations. Let's say the executives are given a fine comprehensive summary each morning. When they reach their work area, on their desks are the summaries they have carefully planned and have had *crafted to meet their needs* (completed staff work) for decision making. They study these and are equipped throughout the day to make what may appear to be snap decisions, but they certainly are not. I'm sure we have the prodigies who are able to make lots of snap decisions and do it well. Even then I think they're lucky if their rate of successful decision making is somewhere in excess of 70 percent.

Question: What about the other kind of manager—the procrastinator who sits and stews and wavers and wobbles and gets a half-decision made and then backs off and goes on another tangent?

Joe: Managers such as you describe are often attempting to be all things to all people. Sometimes they are not working in a "climate for mistakes" where it is understood that normally some mistakes are made. Thus they are not encouraged to cast out into the unknown to innovate or create. I'd like to provide here a few specific suggestions for this kind of manager. We aren't putting them down. We are saying a lot of us need a lot of help in sound, practical decision making. You might call this a comprehensive set of steps to follow. The first might be to assign the best people to make a particular study. Consider what results can be expected and when the project is to be completed. Evaluate the situation and all the known facts. Collect all the additional information needed to make the decision. Present suggested courses of action and estimate the degree of risk connected with each course. Compare these various courses of action with company objectives and resources. Get the best input from your team. Then make the decision. Put the necessary plans into operation and be prepared to review, modify, or reverse action as needed. Of course, this requires that we have closed-loop systems of control set up. We'll be talking more about that. What it really means, in essence, is that it's important to constantly get feedback every hour, or every day, or every month, or even every minute *if* you need it. This feedback indicates to you the effectiveness of your decisions in moving steadily toward a course of objectives or expectations that you have set.

We hear quite a bit of talk about T-group training and sensitivity training. Predictably, I'm often asked what I think of sensitivity training. You see, sensitivity is supposed to be related strongly to decision making. My response is that I think bad sensitivity training is bad and excellent sensitivity training is excellent. That statement produces some pretty blank looks. It should, because it's a pretty blank statement. What I am saying is that there is nothing good or bad about sensitivity training per se. It is how you do it. I believe it should consist of four phases: Analysis, Evaluation, Synthesis, and Synergy.

Analysis means to break a thing into its component parts. When we get a group of people together for sensitivity training, and we focus only on what is wrong with each other, and we quit at that point and everybody goes back home, we go back a little shook up, a little bit traumatized, perhaps a little less a person than when we came.

Now to carry this thing on and make it productive, we must go beyond analysis to evaluation which is to attach value to the components which we came up with when we analyzed the problem or the person. We put these value components together through synthesis so that the whole is greater than the sum of the parts which, of course, is what the word synergy means. Synergy is a term that means you put a couple of elements together and the whole is greater than the sum of the parts.

So people go back from this kind of training with a heightened level of sensitivity about their worth, their strengths, with a heightened level of self-esteem, self-fulfillment, and self-actualization. Their capacity then to move off the dime is very sharply increased. It might seem on a topic like decision making that we are getting away from the subject when we talk about sensitivity training but there are many lists such as I gave a minute ago of things to do to organize and so forth. The all important thing and the difficult thing is to cultivate a *belief in yourself* that enables you then to make courageous decisions and to confront.

Question: It's often said that once the operation is planned and the team is set, that there isn't much need for decisions. That isn't true, is it? Aren't there decisions to be made all along the line?

Joe: All the time. I know of no way that you can organize or legislate to the point where this doesn't happen. Otherwise you begin to destroy viability, and you have a static organization.

Question: An easy way for a young aspiring manager to get in the habit of making decisions and making them quickly is to handle them like a luncheon menu. You are faced with a bill of fare with many choices. The secret is to make up your mind within ten seconds (or perhaps a minute to start with) as to what you will order. Over a period of time you can form a habit of looking the choices over, picking the one you want and get it over with. Although you may not want to. Now you could procrastinate over it indefinitely, but you can train yourself to get into the habit of making the decision within a limited period of time.

Joe: I think that's a good analogy. Each person looks at a menu quite differently. One may be worried about cholesterol, another about carbohydrates, and another about calories. One may be just so hungry he or she wants substantial fare and yet another may be experiencing a touch of indigestion. So, for a whole variety of reasons, all of the values that we place on our daily living, our appearance, our fitness, our visceral feelings at that moment, are all influencing that thing called a decision. No matter how we try to get away from it and say, "Now wait a minute, you can make practical profit-making decisions without all this value business," you simply can't. We are all walking skinfulls of values. It helps to make good decisions if you *feel* good.

Question: There is an old philosophy that has become increasingly popular over the last few years. The freedom that a person possesses to make decisions concerning the course of life is a frightening and, to many people, an almost overwhelming responsibility to eliminate all other courses of action. In other words, once you make a decision to act upon a plan, you decide at the same time, against a whole host of things. That's what makes it so hard, isn't it?

Joe: Things like this sound philosophical and far removed, yet they are a study of everyone's existence in which all are involved whether they've given any conscious thought to it or not.

Question: Is there a scientific way to reach a valid and workable decision?

Joe: I think there are some scientific things we can *do* to approach the *art* of decision making. I am kind of a semantic purist on the "art" and "science" business. Here are some things that I'd like to recommend as we move toward the "state of the art" concerning decision making.

Let's say the persons we are going to describe now are, indeed, space-age executives. I think they should be aware of and dedicated to fulfilling the responsibilities of their position. They should want to be held accountable for their success in achieving the objectives of their company. I'd say they must select people of integrity and intellect to work with them, people who have the ability and desire to meet commitments. Then the executives should hold those people accountable. *Executives must respect their own dignity and the dignity of others.* Certainly this has a fundamental impact on the decisions they make.

Reward accomplishment and give leadership when needed; punish and reprimand if necessary. Executives should provide clear-cut objectives for their department heads that can be followed without constant supervision. They should delegate authority to the lowest level of management capable of making decisions.

Here, again, you see how this ties to completed staff work and management by exception. Executives should remove from their desks all decision making not requiring their time and judgment, at the same time remembering that authority can be delegated but ultimate responsibility remains with them.

They ought to establish communications that not only transmit their requests to subordinates but that keep them fully informed of the results achieved in all components of the organization. Here, again, judgment enters in because we see the one who might be the Empire Builder or Responsibility Reaper who wants to impress the boss with fancy footwork and activity. Vast amounts of data must be fed into this person's desk each day. Only a fraction of this may be needed to determine the right kind of quality of information. I'd suggest four words: Eliminate, Combine, Rearrange, and Simplify. First of all, see what information in the feedback flow of data can be eliminated and then rearrange it, combine it, and simplify it.

A few more things should be done. Establish methods and techniques for studying problems of all types. Here, again, we get into analysis, evaluation, etc. Know and understand the strengths and weaknesses of all resources for which executives are responsible—persons, money, materials, time, and space. Executives must plan for the future, which is coming at us much more quickly than we realize.

I recommend here that executives cultivate, even if they have to calculate this, a zest for the unknown; we might call it Tomorrow-Mindedness. They must understand that change is going to happen anyway and the future is always going to be there. We need to get curious about it, read about it, study about it, think about it, begin to fill our minds here in terms of decision making with pertinent materials, oftentimes very crucial materials, that enable us to make practical decisions about tomorrow. And—remember—real expective managers want the benefit of all logical input from their subordinates possible. We call it consultative decision making.

Question: Aren't most managers fond of the status quo? I think you once said that 80 percent of all managers are obsolete. What do you mean by that?

Joe: Well, I believe they are, but I don't believe they need to remain that way. That's why we're in the business of training managers.

I don't believe managers are really fond of the status quo, but sputter and dwell on the status quo because they don't have the thrust and confidence needed to depart from it. Deep down many executives don't want to remain sitting on their status quos, but they don't know how to depart. This is a fundamental part of what we are talking about here.

The importance of a person's building into the mind a race for innerspace between the ears. Positive values, curious, thirsty, hungry, zestful values enable them to depart with courage from the status quo. Often people don't know how to depart, so they settle for less.

One reason for the high percentage of obsolete managers is that many companies are still carrying out the basic "Ps" of the business—the processes, procedures, practices, in search of profit based on *activities*, not results, in spite of the literature and the lip service. That is *one* reason. Another is we are still largely victims of the belief that a person is not of the higher order of things called a human being. We still cling to the notion that a person is basically an animal. Maslow, and many of us, believe each person is a lot more. We've broken down the elements of our planet to animal, vegetable, and mineral. I may be a voice in the wilderness on this, but I'd like to see the time come soon when we quit referring to people as "animals" in the prosaic sense. Human beings have freedom of choice and the ability to make discriminating choices, which is something that animals do not possess. Animals are creatures that react to food stimuli, fear stimuli, etc. Human beings have a choice to make intellectual choices which removes them distinctly from the animal. There has been too much time lost and money spent on studying what people aren't good at. Let's start studying the successful person, not the unsuccessful.

Question: Modern scientists now seem to believe that the human mind is infinite, that there is no limit at all to achievement.

Joe: I believe this. You're probably familiar with research on the extent to which most human brains are used. By the time a person dies after a long and relatively successful life, the highly successful person uses, develops, and activates up to 10 percent of his or her brain cells. What a challenge to develop the other 90 percent.

Question: Is there any technique you can suggest to help the manager make decisions?

Joe: That is a good question. You have to confront. You have to take chances. We must understand the implications of what I call a climate for mistakes. All people need to understand that if they are doing creative, vigorous, expective, and confrontive things, they'll make some mistakes. It is particularly crucial that we have a well-defined process for utilizing the best input of our team. Expect them to proffer proposals and researched recommendations. Then, *you* decide.

IS THERE
ONE BEST WAY TO
DELEGATE TASKS?

Question: Is delegation still a problem for managers in this enlightened day?

Joe: It certainly is. In fact, the problem seems to be growing. It
may be the most major deficiency in management. If you
visit an average company, you'd get the notion there are
quite a number of indispensable people. I emphatically
believe there aren't indispensable people. Everybody
knows managers who still operate as though they think
everything depends upon them, that refuse to let go, that
hide insecurities behind frequent pious comments such
as "If you want to get a thing done right, you have to do
it yourself." This attitude is neither noble nor practical.
Rather it is often dangerous and pathetic. The ability to
get along without a "boss" is frequently proven very
graphically during a vacation. The company not only
seems to continue along beautifully in the boss's ab-
scence, but frequently operates even better. Think of all the
people formerly in the world who were thought of as
almost indispensable but without whom we are getting
along very well.

Question: Is there any wisdom in not delegating jobs?

Joe: There are some extenuating circumstances in which you
know that the best contribution toward the achievement
of company objectives is something you yourself should
actually execute. Again, that becomes the all-important
criterion.

Effective managers are effective because they know best
how to evoke from their subordinates the best efforts, the
expectations. These managers know the strengths and
motives of their subordinates. When they have a talented

team, there is usually very little reason that they should retain very many things. Their job is to *manage*.

Question: It seems managers frequently get into trouble by insisting that those they choose to do the work must do it in the same way that the managers themselves would do it.

Joe: A management team that repeats a course of action because it has worked before, yet does not have the confidence and the trust to delegate, is not going to be able to take advantage of the potential supply of innovative ideas that may help change the growth and direction of the organization. Competent managers are persons who are listening for this kind of thing. They are looking for, not Responsibility Reapers, but people who want a greater opportunity to make a varied and meaningful contribution to objectives and expectations.

Question: A person joining an organization often hears, "Now let me show you how we do things around here; it's the way it has always been done." The best argument for doing it differently is the fact you have always done it that way before. The good manager is looking for a better way.

Joe: This flies in the face of what I call an absolute and that is the statement that change is an absolute. Change is going to happen anyway, and since it is, we must seek it out, try to anticipate it, relish it, and not try to hold fast so we become worndown and disillusioned.

Question: Have managers always had trouble delegating jobs or authority?

Joe: For at least three thousand years that we know of! I'd like to turn to what we think of as a fine source, although not a normal or standard textbook on management. Many people have called it a master textbook—the *Bible*. Let's look at some excerpts from the *Book of Exodus*. Moses had just led his people out ot Egypt, and a major crisis had passed. Now he was faced with a problem of administration. Fortunately he had a wise old father-in-law named Jethro, who should perhaps be considered the first management consultant on record. Let me quote now from the *Book of Exodus*, Chapter 18, Verses 3–26 inclusive:

> On the morrow, Moses sat to judge the people, and the people stood about Moses from morning until evening. When Moses' father-in-law saw what he

was doing for the people, he said, "What is this you are doing for the people? Why are you sitting alone and all the people stand about you from morning to evening?" And Moses said, "Because the people come to me to inquire of God. When they have a dispute, they come to me, and I decide between a man and his neighbor, and I make them know the statutes of God and his decisions." Moses' father-in-law said to him, "What you are doing is not good. You and the people with you will wear yourselves out, for the thing is too heavy for you. You are not able to perform it alone. Listen now to my voice. I will give you counsel and God be with you. You shall represent the people before God and bring their case to God. You shall teach them the statutes and the decisions and make them know the way in which they must walk and what they must do. Moreover, choose able men from all the people, those who fear God and who are trustworthy and who hate a bribe and place such men over the people as rulers of thousands, of hundreds, of fifties, and of tens. Let them judge the people at all times. *Every great matter they shall bring to you, but in the small matters they shall decide themselves.* It shall be easier for you, and they will bear the burden with you. If you do this, and so God commands you, then you will be able to endure and all these people also will go to their place in peace." So Moses gave heed to the voice of his father-in-law, and did all that he had said. Moses chose able men out of all Israel and made them heads over the people, rulers of thousands, of hundreds, of fifties, and of tens. And they judged the people at all times. Hard cases they brought to Moses but small matters they judged themselves.

I think we'd agree here that Jethro boiled it down beautifully—the essential requirements for modern delegation.

Question:　One thing it says to me is that it is absolutely imperative to delegate when an operation reaches a certain level of quantity or complexity.

Joe:　I certainly think so. If Moses and Jethro considered the need to delegate with the kind of problems they had at that time, I don't think there is anything to apologize for when we recognize the limits of our ability to make the best day-to-day use of our talents.

Question: Isn't *not* delegating indicative of a basic insecurity or lack of confidence and strength?

Joe: I really think it is. It is, above all, *a failure to clarify expectations!* Our management literature should more clearly spell out that many people who somehow delude themselves, who put in abnormally long hours, who refuse to take vacations usually feel a basic insecurity and have a lack of sufficient confidence in other people. If we carry that one step further and make it very clear that the only way you can acquire lots of confidence in others is to have lots of confidence in yourself, I think this would make an invaluable contribution to the process of delegation. Remember the people that you delegate jobs to are people with talents and abilities.

Question: You mentioned earlier that your good friend Joe Powell had some interesting comments on delegation. What did he say?

Joe: All the components of the productivity climate can be present, but if individual purposes, decisiveness, and action are missing, the total potential may be shortchanged. It is basic that people in managerial positions must know how to accumulate pertinent information, weigh and assess the facts, and decide upon a course of action. Yet, too many executives lack either courage or know-how in this regard, and often in their uncertainity, cannot bear the thought that people may be saying that the boss doesn't know the answers. They are afraid to invite appropriate participation. Without the best thinking of your subordinates, you are unfortunately not in the best possible position to make decisions. Without their participation, moreover, and with the poor decisions or procrastination which often follow, you lose their respect and drain off much potential productivity.

The principle of completed staff work, long familiar with the military, plays a powerful role here. This, as we all know, calls for studying a problem and presenting a possible solution to one's superior in such a form that all he or she needs to do is approve or disapprove the recommended course of action. Completed staff work is designed to wean the subordinate of relying on the superior at every stage of the assignment for advice and decision making.

In return for relieving the superior of much nonessential detail, however, it imposes a number of responsibilities on the executive making an assignment, and these are: Before you assign a problem or expectation to anyone, be sure you can define the expectation yourself. *There are no solutions to unknown problems.* If you cannot clearly and concisely state or write the problem at a staff meeting, make it clear who is going to follow up to clarify the problem. You are the quarterback, but the team needs to know the play. Tell the ball carrier what the problem is and what you *expect* him or her to do about it. Communication by administrative osmosis seldom produces much besides confusion and frustration.

Next, contribute your experience. You are the boss because you have superior ability. Share it with your assistants. Tell them what you have learned, or what you think you have learned, about the problem. When you give an assignment, set a target date. Giving an assignment without a target date is like asking a friend to come to dinner "some evening."

Next, be accessible for legitimate progress reports. If you don't want today's answer to yesterday's problem or yesterday's answer to today's problem, it will pay you to take an occasional reading on progress. Steadfastly resist the temptation to do your staff's thinking for them. Give guidance and background information, but make them do their own thinking. Remember that it is their job to furnish proposed solutions. Completed staff work is not panacea, it won't solve all your problems, but it will do these three things: free you from unimportant detail, multiply your executive effectiveness, and make your organization run better.

It boils down to this, to paraphrase Joe Powell: As an executive, you can either develop a splendid set of ulcers or teach your staff to do completed staff work. It takes about the same amount of energy either way.

Question: Someone said a problem defined is half solved, and that is certainly true. Joe Powell has done a great job with that summary of how to delegate. If you are in a job where

	you should delegate and don't, you may very well get sick.

Joe: That is quite literally true. We have seen many instances in which people develop heart attacks, emotional problems, ulcers, these sort of problems, because they simply won't let go. These people who are keeping everything in can't reach out and help growth take place. People who hold all this in will implode.

Question: Are effective delegaters persons who have learned to manage by exception?

Joe: Certainly they cannot manage by exception unless they know how to delegate and carry out either a variation of this precise procedure for completed staff work. By management by exception we mean this. Managers free themselves from activities that require their thinking, actions that don't lead themselves directly toward the accomplishment of profit or some other worthwhile objective that they are being paid to make happen. They give those jobs that make a less direct contribution to objectives to people who have less ability. They keep their minds freed up so they can focus on, with adequate thinking time and research time, the *key profitability opportunities*. Frankly, it is an excellent opportunity for the junior person who wants to become a major executive to work with a person who carries out management by exception effectively. In such a company, and I'm afraid we don't see enough of these, you don't snicker at the person who is sitting with a chair tilted back and who is lost in deep thought. On the contrary, we see people who are able to make key strategic moves, because they have left themselves time, through management by exception, to think and, above all, time to act.

Question: Underlying everything we have said here, is it true that to delegate an important responsibility to someone you must trust him or her implicitly?

Joe: Absolutely. To delegate is literally impossible unless, and until, you develop a strong and sustaining feeling of trust about the person in the mirror. *Then* you will be able to trust others. There is, however, no substitute for clearly *thought through* and *communicated* expectations.

MANAGEMENT MANUAL PAR EXCELLENCE

The general manager of a major division of a large company that operates internationally, was bitter, his complexion sallow, his mouth turned down. "Just give me one good reason why we don't have a lot of enthusiasm and motivation in this division. Hell, I've personally attended all kinds of seminars on motivation, communication, human relations, and you name it. I've made sure we're doing all the right things here. But these lazy clunks just don't react.

"*Enthusiasm,*" he said in a measured, abrasive manner, "is all I'm asking for."

Do you see what was happening? Emerson said, "What you are speaks so loudly, I can't hear what you are saying." And this man was calling for something he simply didn't exemplify. So his leadership was not real; it was not authentic. In short, it was phony. He first had, like all of us, to put *himself* on the hook!

I will attempt to demonstrate that the essence of all modern, valid "principles of motivation and management" were spelled out in the *Sermon on the Mount* by Christ, the toughest-minded and most effective executive of all time. Let's list just a few terms which we hear and use frequently in seminars all over the country. They include

Management by results
Involvement and commitment
Confrontation and interface
Effective communicators
Performance standards
Profitability
Self-discipline
Management by integrity

Job enrichment or high expectations
Management by example
Open-mindedness
Sensitivity and empathy
Positive thinking
Accountability for results
Effective decision making
Build on strengths

There are more of these and, as most readers can probably perceive, a complete book could be written and probably should be on the relationship between these "management principles" and the great repository of cybernetic truths known as the *Sermon on the Mount*. The Leader's Manual par excellence.

MANAGEMENT BY RESULTS?

Isn't this better and more simply said by Christ in the statement, "Wherefore by their fruits ye shall know them"? This implies that the policies, procedures, processes, and practices of an organization should relate recognition and compensation for each individual to his or her *actual performance*—not to color, race, creed, old school ties, physical appearance, and other related trivia.

INVOLVEMENT AND COMMITMENT?

The Beatitudes require nothing less. They are performance standards that permit nothing less than tough-minded inner conviction. Compassion, hard work, discipline, love, confrontation—all are required to even partially fulfill their stretching expectations. You simply cannot make a continuous and vigorous effort to meet these standards without a great amount of involved and committed interaction with your fellow man.

CONFRONTATION AND INTERFACE?

The New Testament is literally loaded with these transactions. Here, for example, is some potent scripture that is saturated with confrontation, interface, and accountability.

Whosoever therefore shall break one of these least
commandments, and shall teach men so, he shall be called the
least in the kingdom of heaven; but whosoever shall do and
teach them the same shall be called great in the kingdom of
heaven. For I say unto you, that except your righteousness shall
exceed the righteousness of the scribes and Pharisees, ye shall
in no case enter the kingdom of heaven.

That's telling it like it is!

EFFECTIVE COMMUNICATION?

We know that one of the principal problems vexing management in
organizations of all kinds is communication. Too much paper, too much
irrelevant conversation, memoranda, correspondence, hinting, "di-
plomacy," and oblique innuendoes. Many management pundits and
practitioners will nod sagely and agree that the solution is to "reduce the
complex to the simple." Christ said, in the great Sermon

But let your communication be, Yea, yea; Nay, nay; for
whatsoever is more than these cometh of evil.

The Phillips Translation states it this way.

Whatsoever you have to say, let your "yes" be a plain "yes"
and your "no" be a plain "no"; anything more than this has a
taint of evil.

Performance standards? How about this?

Be ye therefore perfect, even as your Father which is in heaven
is perfect.

Profitability? Christ is most explicit on this.

Even so every good tree bringeth forth good fruit, but a corrupt
tree bringeth forth evil fruit.

In my book, *Tough-Minded Management,* I developed a phrase
called "Management by Integrity." I can in no way, however, take credit
for the underlying truth which you have just read. The company, school,
family, church, government, or other institution or organization that does
not structure its policies, principles, processes, practices, and procedures on integrity may generate profit or demonstrate profit-ability for
awhile, but ultimately it will crumble. It is built on sand.

Integrity might be likened to a foundation of granite.

> And everyone that heareth these sayings of mine, and doeth them not, shall be likened unto a foolish man, which built his house upon the sand. And the rain descended and the floods came, and the winds blew, and beat upon that house; and it fell, and great was the fall of it.

Experienced, pragmatic management consultants know this to simply be fact.

SELF-DISCIPLINE? MANAGEMENT BY EXAMPLE? POSITIVE LISTENING? OPEN-MINDEDNESS? SENSITIVITY AND EMPATHY?

It is accepted virtually as dogma that these are essential to a highly organized productive and profitable enterprise. Note how beautifully the tough-minded Light of the World presents the distilled and beautiful essence—and the answer—to these needs. Here's the Phillips translation:

> Don't criticize people and you will not be criticized. For you will be judged by the way you criticized others, and the measure you give will be the measure you receive.
>
> Why do you look at the speck of sawdust in your brother's eye and fail to notice the plank in your own? How can you say to your brother, "Let me get the speck out of your eye" when there is a plank in your own? You fraud! Take the plank out of your own eye first, and then you can see clearly enough to remove your brother's speck of dust.

My own pet phrase in this context is, "Whenever you point a finger at someone else, you have three pointing back. Try it!

Build on strengths—Don't dwell on weaknesses! Every experienced competent management consultant knows that a sure path to business or organization oblivion is to think about, talk about, and dwell on *weaknesses* of people and/or things. The positive and successful corollary is to seek out, identify, relate to and *apply* strengths. I submit that Christ is speaking squarely to our frequent dilemma in choosing between these two options when he says

> But I say unto you, Love your enemies, bless them that curse you, do good to them that hate you, and pray for them which despitefully use you, and persecute you.

I'm well aware that many readers may disagree with the meaning I have chosen to place on *these demanding words*. My reply to the dissident would be, "Don't knock it until you've *tried* it, and *tried* it, and *tried* it."

MANAGEMENT BY EXAMPLE?

I've already quoted from Emerson, but Matthew said it even better.

For he taught them as one having authority, and not as the scribes.

Jesus was one with God, and therefore when he spoke, he spoke the Word of Power.

JOB ENRICHMENT OR HIGH EXPECTATIONS?

I have the privilege of speaking at hundreds of occasions of virtually all kinds and am increasingly gratified that speakers are beginning to challenge their audiences to *expect* much from their fellow human beings. My own challenge to an audience often goes like this: "Do you have the guts to expect the *best*—not the worst—from your fellow creature and from life itself?"

And here again, Christ says it so much better than we can.

Ask, and it shall be given to you; seek, and ye shall find; knock, and it shall be opened unto you: for everyone that asketh receiveth; and he that seeketh findeth; and to him that knocketh, it shall be opened.

If we are Christians, we have no business to expect second-rate health, or performance, or compensation, or love, or morals. We are commanded to *expect* and *go after* excellence. What corporate executive or staff can match or top this?

There is time and room to treat only one more of these beautiful and potent instruments available to us daily from God. It concerns the daily need of a troubled and confused world for "a way to go," for direction, moral guidelines—a builtin cybernetic guidance and decision-making system. Literally thousands of books on management, motivation, and leadership have been written. And whether the reader is Christian, Buddhist, Hindu, or a member of one of the other great religions; whether he or she be executive, teacher, minister, artisan, farmer, or homemaker, this sublime precept cuts to the heart of the human condition, and gives us all we need.

Therefore all things whatsoever ye would that men should do to you, do ye even so to them: for this is the law and the prophets.

But wait! There's room for one more! You say you believe in these things, but, after all, you're only *one* person? And what can *one* person do?

Ye are the light of the world. A city that is set on a hill cannot be hid. Neither do men light a candle, and put it under a bushel, but on a candlestick; and it giveth light unto all that are in the house. Let your light so shine before men, that they may see your good works, and glorify your Father which is in heaven.

How's that for the *power of example?*
Will you *do* it?

THE TEN COMMANDMENTS OF
EXPECTIVE LIVING

1. I will confront my possibilities, relish my strengths, and be me.
2. I will study and cultivate health—physically, mentally, and spiritually.
3. I will express gratitude to at least one person every day.
4. I will persist in seeing something fine in every person I meet. I will expect their best.
5. I will dare to admit or recapture my dreams.
6. I will practice positive expectations in every dimension of my life.
7. I will shun self-pity with every ounce of my will.
8. I will lead as I would like to be led.
9. I will let gratitude, forgiveness, and laughter soak into my inmost thoughts.
10. I can become whatever I *decide* to be.

THE TEN COMMANDMENTS OF
EXPECTIVE MANAGEMENT

1. I will *tell* no one. But, I will expect much.
2. The truth is the only thing that sets you free.
3. I will diligently attempt to *be* what I expect of others.

4. I will unleash, unshackle, and be proud of my enthusiasm.

5. I will search for some positive strengths in every person. I will expect each person's best.

6. I will share life, love, and laughter with my team.

7. I know that expectations are the key to all happenings.

8. The best control is a clearly understood expectation.

9. I will plan boldly.

10. I will live my plan.

Table A.1 Performance appraisal sequence and procedure

		Create Necessary Instruments				
Determine need	*Determine purpose*	*Accomplishment record*	*Performance standards*	*Performance rating form*	*Prepare for discussion*	*Conduct appraisal session**
What will it accomplish?	Efficiency	Construct carefully	Careful job analysis	Measure *performance*, not activity or personality characteristics	Understand the employee	Establish rapport
Who needs it?	Morale	Obtain involvement, cooperation, etc.	Relate directly to objectives		Make sure employee receives ample advance notice (leadtime)	Warm-up
Why does it seem needed?	Productivity	Keep current	Listen	Keep it simple		Be specific
What is its relationship to organizational development?	Cost reduction	Positives	Boil down	Relate to standards and objectives	Make sure the time is mutually convenient	Be candid
What is expected?	Dynamism	Negatives	Define	Listen	"Check off" each item on the form	Identify strengths
	Team-building		Discuss	Boil down		Build on strengths
	Synergy		Write down	Define	*Review accomplishment record*	Be a positive listener
	Wage and salary aid		Should deal with concrete, attainable results	Discuss		Be calm, quiet, thorough
	Implement MBO			Write down	Review accomplishment record	Coach, don't advise
	Create more "openness"		Developed jointly		Make sure ample explanation and why is provided	Evaluate performance — not the person
	Stimulate creativity		Statements of basic results	Should contain items relating to concrete, attainable results	Remove all possible causes of advance fear and apprehension	Make sure the rating form is secondary. It is an aid only
	Determine training needs		Clearly worded			
	Evaluate objectives		Should measure both quality and quantity	Units	Determine objectives for interview	Relate performance to personal goals and expectations of the employee
	Promotability		On officially approved form	Volume	Review the basic need of the employee	
	Reassignment		As specific as possible	Dollars	Review Performance Standards	Appraise and discuss development and promotional factors
	Profit contribution			Percentage		
	Clarification of expectations				Continuing activity	Discuss actualization of total talents
					Continuous communication with employee	Agree on ways to implement suggested changes
					Communicate all items going into accomplishment record at time of happening	Set new standards
						Obtain feedback on new expectations and commitments
						Expect the best!

* There should be no discussion of salary during the appraisal process.

Table A.2 Performance expectations

Department _____ Employee _____ Date _____

Job title _____ Supervisor _____

Purpose of position: _____
_____
_____
_____

Key commitments			Standards expected			
	Standard	Weight	Goal	Weight	Excellence	Weight
1.	1.		1.		1.	
2.	2.		2.		2.	
3.	3.		3.		3.	
4.	4.		4.		4.	
5.	5.		5.		5.	
6.	6.		6.		6.	
		50		75		100

BIBLIOGRAPHY

Athos, Anthony G. and Richard T. Pascale, 1982, *The Art of Japanese Management,* New York: Wiley.

Batten, Joe D., 1980, *Beyond Management By Objectives,* (2nd Edition), New York: American Management Association.

_____ , 1972, *The Confidence Chasm,* New York: Parker.

_____ , 1966, *Dare to Live Passionately,* New York: Parker.

_____ , 1965, *Developing A Tough-Minded Climate for Results,* New York: American Management Association.

_____ , 1978, *Tough-Minded Management,* (3rd Edition), New York: American Management Association.

_____ , 1989, *Tough-Minded Leadership,* New York: American Management Association.

Bennis, Warren and Bert Nanus, 1990, *Leaders,* New York: Harper & Row.

Covey, Steven, 1990, *The Seven Habits of Highly Effective People,* New York, Simon & Schuster.

Crosby, Phillip B., 1990, *Leading,* New York: McGraw-Hill.

DePree, Max, 1990, *Leadership Is An Art,* New York: Doubleday.

Drucker, Peter F. 1974, *Management,* New York: Harper and Row.

_____ , 1949, *The New Society,* New York: Harper and Row.

Gardner, John W., 1968, *No Easy Victories,* New York: Harper and Row.

Giblin, Les, 1990, *How to Have Confidence and Power in Dealing With People,* Englewood Cliffs, NJ: Reward Books.

Hay, Louise L., 1984, *You Can Heal Your Life,* Santa Monica, CA: Hay House, Inc.

Horton, Thomas R., 1986, *What Works For Me,* New York: Random House.

Kanter, Rosabeth Moss, 1990, *When Giants Learn to Dance,* New York: Simon & Schuster.

_____ , 1987, *The Changemasters,* New York: Simon & Schuster.

Kirkpatrick, Donald L., 1985, *How to Manage Change Effectively,* San Francisco: Jossey-Bass, Inc.

Loden, Marilyn, 1985, *Feminine Leadership,* New York: Time Books.

Manning, Gerald and Barry Reece, 1990, *Selling Today,* Boston: Allyn and Bacon.

Morrisey, George L., 1980, *Getting Your Act Together,* New York: John Wiley & Sons.

Naisbitt, John and Patricia Aburdene, 1990, *Megatrends 2000,* New York: William Morrow & Company.

Nanus, Bert, 1990, *The Leader's Edge,* Chicago: Contemporary Books.

Peale, Norman Vincent, 1974, *You Can If You Think You Can,* Englewood Cliffs, NJ: Prentice-Hall.

_____ , 1952, *The Power of Positive Thinking,* New York: Prentice Hall.

Peters, Tom, 1984, *Passion For Excellence,* New York: Random House.

Perez, Rosita, 1983, *The Music Is You,* Granville, Ohio: Trudy Knox, Publisher.

Randolph, Robert M., 1982, *Thank God It's Monday,* New York: Institute for Business Planning.

Roberts, Wes, 1990, *Leadership Secrets of Atilla the Hun,* New York: Warner Books.

Safir, William and Leonard Safir, 1990 *Leadership,* New York: Simon & Schuster.

Schuller, Robert H., 1980, *The Peak to Peek Principle,* New York: Doubleday and Company.

_____ , 1983, *Tough-Minded Faith for Tender-Hearted People,* Nashville: Thomas Nelson, Inc.

Waitley, Dennis, Dr., 1990, *Seeds of Greatness,* New York: Pocket Books.

Walker, Mary, 1989, *Ready & Willing,* Tulsa: Honor Books.

Waterman, Robert H., Jr., 1988, *The Renewal Factor,* New York: Bantam Books.

Ziglar, Zig, 1978, *Confessions of a Happy Christian,* Gretna, Louisiana: Pelican Publishing Co.

_____ , 1990, *Top Performance,* New York: Berkley Books.

RECOMMENDED VIEWING FROM

The Batten Group
808 Fifth Avenue
Des Moines, Iowa 50309

Joe Batten Videos

Tough-Minded Leadership

Keep Reaching

When Commitments Aren't Met

Solving Employee Conflict

Power-Packed Selling: The Trust Factor in Customer Relationships

The Face-to-Face Payoff, Dynamics of the Interview

The Nuts and Bolts of Performance Appraisal

I Understand—You Understand: The Dynamics of Transactional Analysis

The ABCs of Decision Making

A Recipe for Results: Making Management by Objectives Work

No-Nonsense Delegation

The Nuts and Bolts of Health-Care Management Communication

Tough-Minded Interpersonal Communication for Law Enforcement

Evaluating the Performance of Law Enforcement Personnel

Creating a Tough-Minded Culture

Tough-Minded Supervision for Law Enforcement

Commitment Pays Off

Friendly Persuasion

Keep on Reaching

Trust Your Team

Joe Batten Films/Videos

Ask For the Order and Get It (Dartnell—Chicago, Illinois)

Your Price is Right, Sell It (Dartnell)

Manage Your Time to Build Your Territory (Dartnell)

When You're Turned Down . . . Turn On (Dartnell)

Your Sales Presentation . . . Make It a Winner (Dartnell)

Management by Example (BNA—Rockville, Maryland)

The Man in the Mirror (BNA)

The Fully Functioning Individual (BNA)

The Fully Functioning Organization (BNA)

The Fully Functioning Society (BNA)

RECOMMENDED LISTENING

Audio Cassettes From The Batten Group

How to Apply the Tough-Minded, Decision-Making Process
The Nuts and Bolts of Health Care Management Communication
Tough-Minded Supervision for Law Enforcement
How to Install a Tough-Minded Performance Appraisal System
Joe Batten on Management
The Greatest Secret
Face-to-Face Motivation
Face-to-Face Management
Secrets of Tough-Minded Winners
How to Exceed Yourself

From Other Sources

Closing the Sale, Dave Yogo, General Cassette
The Creative Thinking System, Mike Vance, General Cassette
Prescription for the Happy Life—Refilled, Dr. Charles Jarvis, General Cassette
Living With Stresss Successfully, Dr, Ken Olson, General Cassette
Nonverbal Communication, Dr. Dorothy Shaffer, General Cassette
Telephone Techniques for Secretaries and Receptionists, Thom Norman,
   General Cassette
The Psychology of Winning, Dennis Waitley, Ph.D., Nightingale-Conant

COMPUTERIZED SOFTWARE
FROM THE BATTEN GROUP

CRISP: Computerized Response Individual Strengths Profile
CREAM: Computerized Response Employee Attitude Measurement
CLAMS: Computer Led Automated Marketing Systems
CAI: Computer Aided Interviewing

COMPLIMENTARY
BUSINESS OR PERSONAL NEEDS ANALYSIS
APPLICATION FORM

To secure a telephone appointment for a complimentary analysis of your organization, complete the following form by PRINTING the information requested, and return same along with a self-addressed stamped envelope to:

The Batten Group
808 Fifth Avenue
Des Moines, IA 50309

or call or fax:

The Batten Group
Telephone 1-800-234-3176
Fax 1-515-244-3178

Yes, I have read *Expectations & Possibilities*, and I would like to participate in a complimentary analysis of my organization.

My name is: _____

My business name is: _____

My home address is: Street _____

City _____ State _____ Zip _____

My home phone is: (   )_____

My business phone is: (   )_____

My FAX is: (   )_____

My business is ( ) Sole Proprietorship ( ) Family Business ( ) Partnership ( ) Corporation ( ) Other _____

Describe your organization's products and services:

_____

_____

_____

My position is: _____

My key business concerns are: ( ) Not enough time ( ) Not enough revenue ( ) Not enough profit ( ) Not enough personal income ( ) Productivity and performance of my people is disappointing ( ) Other _____

_____

_____